theatre & audience

D0755417

Theatre &

Series Editors: Jen Harvie and Dan Rebellato

Published

Colette Conroy: *Theatre & the Body*
Jill Dolan: *Theatre & Sexuality*
Helen Freshwater: *Theatre & Audience*
Jen Harvie: *Theatre & The City*
Nadine Holdsworth: *Theatre & Nation*
Erin Hurley: *Theatre & Feeling*
Joe Kelleher: *Theatre & Politics*
Ric Knowles: *Theatre & Interculturalism*
Caoime McAvinchey: *Theatre & Prison*
Helen Nicholson: *Theatre & Education*
Lionel Pilkington: *Theatre & Ireland*
Paul Rae: *Theatre & Human Rights*
Dan Rebellato: *Theatre & Globalization*
Nicholas Ridout: *Theatre & Ethics*

Forthcoming

Susan Bennet: *Theatre & Museums*
Dominic Johnson: *Theatre & the Visual*
Bruce McConachie: *Theatre & Mind*
Juliet Rufford: *Theatre & Architecture*
Rebecca Schneider: *Theatre & History*
Susan Bennett: *Theatre & Museums*

Theatre& Series
Series Standing Order

ISBN 978–0–333–230–20327–3
You can receive future titles in this series as they are published by placing a standing order.
Please contact your bookseller or, in case of difficulty, write to us at the address below with
your name and address, the title of the series and the ISBN quoted above.
Customer Services Department, Macmillan Distribution Ltd Houndmills, Basingstoke,
Hampshire RG21 6XS, England

theatre & audience

Helen Freshwater

palgrave
macmillan

© Helen Freshwater 2009
Foreword © Lois Weaver 2009

All rights reserved. No reproduction, copy or transmission of this publication may be made without written permission.

No portion of this publication may be reproduced, copied or transmitted save with written permission or in accordance with the provisions of the Copyright, Designs and Patents Act 1988, or under the terms of any licence permitting limited copying issued by the Copyright Licensing Agency, Saffron House, 6-10 Kirby Street, London EC1N 8TS.

Any person who does any unauthorized act in relation to this publication may be liable to criminal prosecution and civil claims for damages.

The author has asserted her right to be identified as the author of this work in accordance with the Copyright, Designs and Patents Act 1988.

First published 2009 by
PALGRAVE MACMILLAN

Palgrave Macmillan in the UK is an imprint of Macmillan Publishers Limited, registered in England, company number 785998, of Houndmills, Basingstoke, Hampshire RG21 6XS.

Palgrave Macmillan in the US is a division of St Martin's Press LLC, 175 Fifth Avenue, New York, NY 10010.

Palgrave Macmillan is the global academic imprint of the above companies and has companies and representatives throughout the world.

Palgrave® and Macmillan® are registered trademarks in the United States, the United Kingdom, Europe and other countries.

ISBN-13: 978-0-230-21028-8 paperback
ISBN-10: 0-230-21028-7 paperback

This book is printed on paper suitable for recycling and made from fully managed and sustained forest sources. Logging, pulping and manufacturing processes are expected to conform to the environmental regulations of the country of origin.

A catalogue record for this book is available from the British Library.

A catalog record for this book is available from the Library of Congress.

10 9 8 7 6 5 4 3
18 17 16 15 14 13 12 11

Printed and bound in China

contents

Series editors' preface   vii

Foreword by Lois Weaver   ix

Difficulties of definition   5

Models and frames   11

The road less travelled   27

Suspicion, frustration, and contempt   38

Potent orthodoxies   55

Playing with the audience   62

Further reading   77

Index   85

series editors' preface

The theatre is everywhere, from entertainment districts to the fringes, from the rituals of government to the ceremony of the courtroom, from the spectacle of the sporting arena to the theatres of war. Across these many forms stretches a theatrical continuum through which cultures both assert and question themselves.

Theatre has been around for thousands of years, and the ways we study it have changed decisively. It's no longer enough to limit our attention to the canon of Western dramatic literature. Theatre has taken its place within a broad spectrum of performance, connecting it with the wider forces of ritual and revolt that thread through so many spheres of human culture. In turn, this has helped make connections across disciplines; over the past fifty years, theatre and performance have been deployed as key metaphors and practices with which to rethink gender, economics, war, language, the fine arts, culture and one's sense of self.

Theatre & is a long series of short books which hopes to capture the restless interdisciplinary energy of theatre and performance. Each book explores connections between theatre and some aspect of the wider world, asking how the theatre might illuminate the world and how the world might illuminate the theatre. Each book is written by a leading theatre scholar and represents the cutting edge of critical thinking in the discipline.

We have been mindful, however, that the philosophical and theoretical complexity of much contemporary academic writing can act as a barrier to a wider readership. A key aim for these books is that they should all be readable in one sitting by anyone with a curiosity about the subject. The books are challenging, pugnacious, visionary sometimes and, above all, clear. We hope you enjoy them.

Jen Harvie and Dan Rebellato

foreword: a rapture kept secret

Reading *Theatre & Audience*, I remembered sitting in a matinee audience for David Hare's *The Secret Rapture* at the National Theatre in London with my Split Britches theatre-making partner, Peggy Shaw. I was drawn there by the title, not for its associations with the Christian love affair with death or the end of time, but by the exquisite idea of a *rapture* kept *secret*. Peggy was there under duress. She 'doesn't like plays', but agreed to keep me company. We took our seats in the middle of the stalls surrounded by theatregoers who seemed to have spent a lifetime loving plays and for whom this was one matinee among many. *The Secret Rapture* is a story of personal struggle set against the political backdrop of Thatcher's Britain. This was familiar. It was 1988 and we had set out our own struggles against Reagan's America in Split Britches' latest performance, *Upwardly Mobile Home*.

The play began and we all settled into a quiet attention that might have been mistaken for a collective nap after lunch but was most likely a collective understanding of the political commentary of Hare's story and a shared empathy for his heroine's dilemma.

Then, near the end, in Act 2 Scene 3, the heroine's obsessed and rejected lover manages to get into her flat. He produces a gun. We, the collective viewer, know something bad is going to happen. We, the over-sensitised and theatrically jaded feminist theatre-makers, know that HE is going to rape HER or kill HER or both. He puts the gun on the table near where she is standing and steps back. The gun is easily within HER reach, and yet we all know SHE's the one who will die. At this point Peggy shouts, literally raises her voice above this sea of the well behaved, and shouts, 'Pick up the gun and shoot the bastard!' There is a collective but silent intake of breath; nothing moves except the hairs on the backs of necks. Gripped by a desperate need for decorum, I give Peggy a familial kick and whisper, 'If nothing else, think of the actors!' There's a cautious exhale, then everything goes as planned. HE picks up the gun and kills HER.

This moment of being caught between individual responsibility and collective response, between active engagement and passive consumption, is my lived experience of Helen Freshwater's careful survey of the wide range of approaches that theatre scholars, philosophers, practitioners and promoters take when considering the presence and power of the audience. It is also a reply to her call for more research that explores audience response. We each have our own rapture, whether we sit politely in the company of pearls and suits on a Saturday afternoon or offer vocal and daring alternatives; whether we swallow it whole or read between the lines; whether we rage against the critic who saw the performance as a series of in-jokes because everyone seemed to get it but him or stay home because the reviews are bad; whether we hold an ice cube mouth-to-mouth with a performer until our lips meet or hold season tickets to our local regional theatre. Our individual raptures are likely to be kept secret.

Unless, as Helen Freshwater aptly suggests, someone bothers to ask: What did you make of that?

Go on, ask.

Lois Weaver is Professor of Contemporary Performance Practice at Queen Mary University of London and a performance artist, writer, director and activist. She co-founded Spiderwoman Theatre, Split Britches Company and the WOW Theatre in New York, and was Artistic Director of Gay Sweatshop Theatre in London.

theatre & audience

> You are the topic. ... You are the centre. You are
> the occasion. You are the reasons why.
>
> Peter Handke, *Offending the Audience*
> (1966, p. 21)

The presence of an audience is central to the definition of theatre, and the twentieth century saw an explosion of interest in the audience's role among experimental theatre practitioners. In 1968, Peter Brook insisted in *The Empty Space* – a text that is now a well-worn touchstone in theatre studies – that he could 'take any empty space and call it a bare stage', observing: 'A man walks across this empty space whilst someone else is watching him, and this is all that is needed for an act of theatre to be engaged' (p. 11). In the same year Jerzy Grotowski defined theatre as 'what takes place between spectator and actor' in *Towards a Poor Theatre* (p. 32). Writing in 1999, Tim Etchells encouraged his readers to contemplate the 'irreducible fact of theatre – actors and an audience to whom they must speak' (*Certain Fragments*, p. 94). The theatrical experiments carried out by these directors and many other practitioners during the twentieth century have shown us that theatre is not dependent upon its location in a designated building or institution and that it is possible to do away with plot, character, costumes, set, sound, and script. As Handke's characters acknowledge in *Offending the Audience* (Theater am Turm, Frankfurt, 1966), the relationship with the audience provides the theatre event with its rationale. This relationship is indispensable.

This indispensability does not mean that audiences have always been treated with deference or that they have been allowed to watch or listen undisturbed, as the title of Handke's play indicates. The desire to reconfigure the relationship between theatre and its audiences was a recurring theme in experimental theatre practice during the twentieth century and continues to preoccupy many practitioners, and these attempts to reposition the audience have proceeded as much by castigation as they have by celebration. In fact, the polemic which surrounds audiences – and the concerns and anxieties which have been projected onto them from both outside and inside the theatre – seem to be generated by a complex mix of hope, frustration, and disgust.

Some of these attitudes are apparent in the terms that are often used to describe audiences and their behaviour. Take the word 'spectator', for example. Do spectators simply watch? Or are they gazing, or gawking? Are they impartial observers, innocent bystanders, or voyeurs? The terms employed to describe audiences and their relationship to performance are laden with value judgements. Are they just viewers, or accomplices, witnesses, participants? Are they a crowd, a mass, a mob, or critics and connoisseurs? In this book, I want to interrogate some of the assertions, prejudices, and polemic which continue to shape our attitudes towards audience in order to explore how these produce our sense of what theatre is, has been, and should be.

Examining the discourse relating to theatre audiences can also help us understand the hopes, expectations, and frustrations which surround other cultural forms which position us as part of a collective. Our sense of the proper, or ideal, relationship between theatre and its audiences can illuminate our hopes for other models of social interaction, clarifying our expectations of community, democracy, and citizenship, and our perception of our roles and power (or lack of it) within the broader public sphere. As Susan Bennett puts it in her preface to the updated 1997 edition of her *Theatre Audiences* (a book which has become a central reference point in the field): '[T]he act of theatre-going can be a significant measure of what culture affords to its participants' (p. vii). This quotation signals Bennett's investment in one of the most cherished orthodoxies in theatre studies: the belief in a connection between audience participation and political empowerment. In what follows, I want to ask some uncomfortable questions about this belief. For example: why, when there is so much to suggest that the responses of theatre audiences are rarely unified or stable, do theatre scholars seem to be more comfortable making strong assertions about theatre's unique influence and impact upon audiences than gathering and assessing the evidence which might support these claims? Why do they appear to prefer discussing their own responses, or relaying the opinions of reviewers, to asking 'ordinary' theatre-goers – with no professional stake in the theatre – what they make of a performance? Could this apparent aversion to engaging with audience response be related to deep-seated suspicion of, and frustration with, audiences? And, if so, what are the grounds for this suspicion? Why are audiences apparently not to be trusted?

A word, before I continue, about the scope and focus of this book. It concentrates on productions which I have experienced personally and on work which is well documented by others and has generated broader critical debate within theatre and performance studies. This means that it focuses upon canonical European and North American theatre and its audiences in the twentieth and twenty-first centuries, with a particular bias towards contemporary British performance, which has seen an extraordinary increase in the use of audience participation since the turn of the millennium. My responses to the performances I describe below are also strongly informed by the British political scene. Since New Labour's election under Tony Blair in 1997, we have seen ongoing governmental interest in the concept and potentials of participation, reflected in public policies which aim to increase the electorate's engagement with the democratic system and local government, and in education and arts policies directed at widening participation and reaching new audiences. In this context the questions I want to raise about the connections between collective experience, audience participation, political agency, and 'the people' have a particular urgency.

Difficulties of definition: the communal situation

Several barriers block a better understanding of the relationship between theatre and its audiences. One is the tendency to confuse individual and group response; another is the persistent circulation of exaggerated and unsubstantiated claims about theatre's influence and impact. But let's start with the challenges presented by the term 'audience' itself. The word's origins in the Latin verb *audire* – 'to hear' – suggest that audiences have been thought of primarily as listeners, rather than viewers, at certain moments in the past. This seems to be at odds with the emphasis in the roots of the ancient word for theatre, which translates as 'place of seeing', and indicates that historical shifts occur in our understanding of which senses audiences are predominantly using at performances. Even more significant problems are generated by the term's association with an assembled group. The common tendency to refer to an audience as 'it' and, by extension, to think of this 'it' as a single entity, or a collective, risks obscuring the multiple contingencies of subjective response, context, and environment which condition an individual's interpretation of a particular performance event. A confident description of a singular audience reaction may do no justice at all to the variety of response among different members of that audience. So it is important to remember that each audience is made up of individuals who bring their own cultural reference points, political beliefs, sexual preferences, personal histories, and immediate preoccupations to their interpretation of a production. Regular theatre-goers know that post-show discussions reveal how widely responses can vary, even among friends who might be expected to bring similar ideological perspectives and cultural experiences to the event.

What's more, these differences are present within individuals as well as among them. It is possible to find yourself judging and responding to a production in a number of different – and potentially conflicting – ways, as Alice Rayner points out in her essay 'The Audience: Subjectivity, Community and the Ethics of Listening' (1993). Rayner articulates the different subject positions she occupies: 'Sometimes I hear you from my position as a woman, sometimes as a professor, sometimes as a mother, sometimes as bourgeois' (p. 4). Rayner's list is a useful reminder that a single person can experience multiple responses to a show which may well be at odds with one another. Nevertheless, for performers, the need to negotiate the reality of encountering a group of spectators, gathered together with the intent of watching their show, remains a pressing issue, regardless of the fragility, contingency, or transience of that audience's collective identity (or indeed the internal debates which individual audience members may entertain). Tim Etchells, director of Sheffield-based performance ensemble Forced Entertainment – whose performances often draw attention to the relationship between performers and spectators – reflects on the tension between awareness of the differences among spectators and the collective experience of theatre-going in *Programme Notes* (a collection edited by Daniel Brine and Lois Kiedan, 2007):

> Watching the best theatre and performance we are together and alone. Together in the sense that we're aware of the temporary and shifting bonds that link us both to the stage and to our fellow watchers, plugged into the group around and in front of us, the communal situation, sensing the laughter, attentiveness, tension or unease that grip us collectively, in waves and ripples, in jolts, jumps and uncertain spirals or in other forma-tions that do not yet have a name. Sat watching we spread-out, osmose, make connections. But at the same time, even as we do so, we feel our separateness, our difference from those around us, from those on-stage. Even as we shift and flow within the group, we're aware that our place in its emerging consensus, its temporary community, is partial and provisional – that in any case the group itself – there in the theatre, as elsewhere, in our cities and streets, in the relations between nations, peoples and states – is always as much a fraught and necessary question, a longing and a problem, as it is any kind of certainty. (p. 26)

Etchells's portrait of the complex paradoxes inherent in being an audience member usefully indicates what is at stake in our understanding of the nature of community and collective experience. His description of the experience of connection occurring through a process of osmosis reflects long-standing hypotheses about how beliefs and behaviour spread among mass gatherings, groups, and crowds, but his sense of the limitations of communal experience has a specifically twenty-first century inflection. Etchells's awareness that community is temporary and provisional – as much a matter of problematic and frustrated desire as it is a tangible reality – chimes with concerns about who 'we' are in an age of terrorism and swiftly shifting populations and sites of wealth. After all, in many of today's urban centres it is impossible to be sure that the people you live, travel, or work alongside – and those whom you sit next to in the theatre – share your language, your sense of national identity, or indeed any of your beliefs. An assumption that they do so may cause confusion, misunderstanding, or even offence.

Unfortunately, not everyone is as alert as Etchells to the potential problems with an assumption that every member of a crowd or an audience feels the same way. As Elin Diamond points out in her essay 'The Violence of "We": Politicizing Identification' (1991), traditional theatre reviews often blithely ignore the possibility of a range of audience response, as their writers make assertions such as 'we feel Macbeth's fear' or 'we understand Nora's frustration'. The trouble with these statements is the way they project the subjective responses of the critic on to the rest of the audience, discursively producing the audience the critic would like to imagine rather than accurately reflecting the complexity and potential diversity of collective and individual response. As Diamond observes, 'One of the effects of such rhetoric (in which the emotions and thoughts of others are assumed to follow our model) is a fictitious but powerful sense of community that buttresses but also conceals the narcissistic claims of the critic' (p. 404). Of course, this fiction is exposed when the judgements of reviewers are plainly out of kilter with those of audiences. It is especially obvious when reviewers condemn a show yet simultaneously record its enthusiastic reception by other audience members. For example, Miguel Piñero's prison drama *Short Eyes* (The Theater of the Riverside Church, New York, 1973) was panned when it transferred to Broadway. In 'Seeing Ethnicity' (which appears in Thomas Fahy and Kimball King's 2003 collection *Captive Audience: Prison and Captivity in Contemporary Theater*) Fiona Mills argues that this critical attack was the product of racial and class-based prejudices, as reviewers implied not only that the author (a Puerto Rican former convict) was 'ignorant and unsophisticated' but also that the loud, active engagement of the play's racially diverse audience was both 'inappropriate' and 'offensive' (pp. 42, 47). This critical censure of an appreciative, engaged audience speaks volumes about the snobbery and racism that could be found among reviewers of the period; it also serves as a useful reminder of the acts of ideological exclusion which may be realised through assertions about audience response. So, although it is possible to speak of 'an audience', it is important to remember that there may be several distinct, co-existing audiences to be found among the people gathered together to watch a show and that each individual within this group may choose to adopt a range of viewing positions. Moreover, awareness of these differences requires that statements about audience response be framed in careful, conditional terms, sensitive to tendencies to generalise about audiences and to judge them without evidence.

Of course, this caution may well be anathema to many who feel strongly about theatre and its potential to move those who witness it. The desire to promote theatre often results in remarkable claims. For example, Iain Mackintosh's conclusion to *Architecture, Actor and Audience* (1992), 'Unfolding a Mystery', states that the primary purpose of theatre architecture is 'to provide a channel for energy'. He continues:

> Although this energy flows chiefly from performer
> to audience the performer is rendered impotent
> unless he or she receives in return a charge from
> the audience. This can be laughter in a farce, a
> shared sense of awe in a tragedy and even a physical reciprocity to the achievement of dancer or
> actor. The energy must flow both ways so that
> the two forces fuse together to create an ecstasy
> which is comparable only to that experienced in a
> religious or sexual encounter. (p. 172)

Mackintosh's extraordinary assertions have much to tell us about his commitment to theatre and about the strength of cultural belief in the uniqueness of live performance. But they provide little information about what is really going on between theatre and its audiences. A more precise analysis of audience response will have to be sought elsewhere.

Models and frames: readership, spectatorship, embodiment, and affect

What a review of the existing literature quickly reveals is that academic publications which address the question of theatre audiences exclusively and directly are relatively few and far between. The tendency to surround theatre's affective impact in mystifying mythology – together with the difficulties of doing justice to the fleeting phenomenon of collective and individual audience response – may help to explain this dearth. But this scarcity still seems surprising, given that the presence of a witness or watcher is central to most definitions of performance, and it is particularly striking in light of the voluminous literature which covers audience response in television and film studies. The analysis of audience response in theatre studies has lagged behind these disciplines methodologically, as well. Writing in 1989, Marvin Carlson observed in 'Theatre Audiences and the Reading of Performance' that theatre studies had yet to engage with the broader intellectual shift from literary theories which looked to the text as the ultimate source of meaning. He noted that 'much theatre theory still regards the theatre performance as something created and set before an essentially passive audience', and he argued that this traditional model failed to consider 'how that audience learns to respond ... or what demands and contributions it brings to the event' (p. 82). Carlson suggested that this neglect could be remedied through the greater application of the work of reader response theoreticians, such as Hans Robert Jauss, Wolfgang Iser, Umberto Eco, and Stanley Fish.

Susan Bennett's *Theatre Audiences* – first published in 1990 and revised in 1997 – met the need that Carlson identified. Bennett's monograph focused upon performances which had attempted to address marginalised and non-traditional audiences since the 1960s. It was the first – and at the time of writing only – book-length attempt to apply literary reader response theories and theories of spectatorship to the analysis of theatre audiences and is now virtually omnipresent as a reference point in the field. Bennett touches upon the work of Eco, Jauss, Iser, and Fish, as well as that of French cultural theorist Roland Barthes. Barthes's essay 'The Death of the Author' (1968), reprinted in *Image–Music–Text* (1977), argues that critics should stop basing their analysis of literature upon the information they have about 'the author, his person, his life, his tastes, his passions' (p. 143) and that they should focus instead upon the work of interpretation being done by the reader and consider how their understanding of the meaning of an individual text is dependent upon a broader 'intertextual' network. Applying this theory to theatre implies a shift in emphasis from preoccupation with the biography and intention of the playwright or director towards interrogation of the frames of reference which the audience brings to a show.

Bennett also uses the theories of American literary scholar Stanley Fish to explore this idea. In *Is There a Text in This Class?* (1980), Fish argues that the perceived value of a text is a product of the shared interpretive strategies of the community which passes judgement upon it, rather than qualities intrinsic to the text. Bennett applies this theory of 'interpretive communities' to the critical response to Harold Pinter's *The Birthday Party*, which was slated by the reviewer for *The Times* after its premiere at the Lyric Hammersmith in London in 1958, whereas previews of the same production had been enthusiastically received in Oxford and Cambridge. Bennett attributes this divergence in opinion to the likelihood that the academic communities in Oxford and Cambridge were more familiar with the traditions of the European avant-garde that informed Pinter's work. She goes on to demonstrate that the values of interpretive communities shift and change over time, citing a fulsome 1964 review of *The Birthday Party* that also appeared in *The Times*, which asserted that the play was 'the Ur-text of modern British drama' (p. 41).

Theatre Audiences also explores theories of spectatorship developed in film studies. Bennett focuses on feminist film theorists who are interested in critiquing the gender politics of mainstream cinema. She foregrounds Laura Mulvey's hugely influential essay 'Visual Pleasure and Narrative Cinema' (1975, reprinted in *Visual and Other Pleasures*, 1989), which explores the voyeuristic pleasures afforded by classical, narrative-driven films, which cater – according to Mulvey – to a hypothetical male spectator inasmuch as female characters are presented not only as objects of a narrative drive but also as visual objects; passive, sexualised, and subject to the active male gaze. Mulvey's essay has attracted substantial criticism, however. Some critics have argued that its emphasis upon gender is problematically universalised; that it fails to take into account the perhaps more significant differences of nationality, ethnicity, and class. Others have questioned whether the voyeurism central to her critique of the male gaze still applies if technology provides spectators with many more choices about what they watch or even allows them to make creative interventions into content. For example, Elizabeth Klaver's 'Spectatorial Theory in the Age of Media Culture' (1995) suggests that the voyeuristic, gendered, and authoritative gaze posited by Mulvey in the 1970s no longer corresponds to the range of viewing experiences available in television, film, and drama. Her reading of Megan Terry's *Brazil Fado* (Magic Theatre, Omaha, 1977) contends that the play's evocation of the experience of watching television – complete with regular interruption by commercials and the constant displacement of images achieved by channel hopping – 'ripped up' this form of spectatorial theory (p. 295). Klaver's observations are only strengthened by the latest developments in digital technology, which have had a profound effect on the music, film, and communications industries, producing levels of interaction and choice that would have been all but unimaginable in the 1970s.

Developments in technology and the speed of change in the media environment may quickly make standing debates in audience research obsolete, but there may be more substantial problems with using concepts, principles, and theoretical models to analyse theatre that were originally generated in response to reading, writing, or watching film. Bennett acknowledges that the neglect of the specificities of theatre-going by reader response theorists is 'at once liberating and frustrating' (*Theatre Audiences*, p. 20), as these models inevitably fail to reflect the unique characteristics of the theatre experience: the possibility that the response of the audience may influence the delivery of the performance, the live presence of spectators and performers in shared time and space. Other theatre scholars are well aware of these limitations. Despite regular references to 'readers' and 'readings' of performance, it is clear that there are profound differences between the private perusal of a book and the experience of attending a performance. Marvin Carlson, for example, reflects on responses to performances which displease or offend in 'Theatre Audiences and the Reading of Performance'. He notes that 'a frustrated reader may simply put the book aside and turn to something else. The theatre, as a social event, encourages more active resistance' (pp. 85–6) – or more frustrated submission, as the case may be.

Others have proposed that more fundamental assumptions about theatre spectatorship require reassessment. Philosopher Jacques Rancière argues in his lecture 'The Emancipated Spectator' (delivered at the Fifth International Summer Academy of Arts in Frankfurt in 2004 and then published in 2007) that we need to reconfigure completely the theoretical presuppositions and political beliefs that govern discussion of theatre, performance, and spectatorship and to do away with the idea that 'spectatorship is a bad thing'

(p. 272). In this lecture he suggests that twentieth-century proposals for reform of the theatre which sought to trouble the presumed passivity of the spectator were based upon a set of long-established – but problematic and redundant – associations and oppositions, namely, 'the equivalence of theatre and community, of seeing and passivity, of externality and separation, of mediation and simulacrum; the opposition of collective and individual, image and living reality, activity and passivity, self-possession and alienation' (p. 274).

Undoing these connections and divisions is a major task – one that, as Rancière puts it, requires nothing less than tackling a 'dramaturgy of guilt and redemption', as these new forms of theatre become the battleground between 'the evil of the spectacle and the virtue of the true theatre' (p. 274). Rancière concentrates his efforts upon challenging what he sees as the misguided tendency to link seeing and passivity, as he asserts that the act of watching should not be equated with intellectual passivity. This conclusion is based upon his earlier work on theories of pedagogy, and he compares theatre practitioners who believe that audiences need to learn to replace passive viewing with more active forms of engagement to teachers who depend for their authority upon a presumption of ignorance on the part of the student. Rancière argues that such beliefs and presumptions are essentially undemocratic. Instead we should assume that teachers and students – or artists and spectators – are equally intelligent and capable of intellectual discrimination. He encourages us to reflect upon the work of interpretation that each audience member is engaged in, observing: 'Spectatorship is not a passivity that must be turned into activity. It is our normal situation. We learn and teach, we act and know, as spectators who link what they see with what they have seen and told, done and dreamed' (p. 277).

This shift in attitude has long been under way in theatre and performance. Although Rancière's challenge to the ingrained connection between passivity and spectatorship is invaluable, his reading of theatre practice – limited as it is to Antonin Artaud and Bertolt Brecht – presumes a determinism among directors and dramaturges which has in many ways passed. In fact, a plethora of theatrical work now foregrounds the need for active interpretation on the part of the spectator, as it requires observers to make their own decisions about the significance of actions or symbolic material. For example, the influential New York-based company the Wooster Group – in productions such as *Route 1 & 9 (The Last Act)* (1981), *L.S.D. (... Just the High Points...)* (1984), and *Brace Up!* (1991), all first performed at the Performing Garage, New York – have specialised in jazz-like montages of diverse material. David Savran's account of the company's work in *Breaking the Rules* (1988) highlights the way their productions require that the spectator

> make the kind of choices usually considered the province of the writer and/or performer. As a result, each piece must be considered only partially composed when it is presented to the public, not because it is unfinished, but because it requires an audience to realise the

multitude of possibilities on which it opens. As each spectator, according to his part, enters into a dialogue with the work, the act of interpretation becomes a performance, an intervention in the piece. (p. 55)

If the assumption that looking is a necessarily passive activity requires challenging, then perhaps we also need to consider whether it is useful to place such emphasis upon a single sense. After all, audience members bring their whole bodies with them into the auditorium, not just their eyes. As Simon Shepherd puts it in *Theatre, Body and Pleasure* (2006), 'Theatre is an art of bodies witnessed by bodies' (p. 73). Shepherd highlights historical instances of this awareness and cites Bernard Beckerman's *The Dynamics of Drama* (1970), which encouraged its readers to consider the 'muscular tension' experienced by audience members:

Although theater response seems to derive principally from visual and aural perception, in reality it relies upon a totality of perception that could be better termed kinesthetic. We are aware of a performance through varying degrees of concentration and relaxation within our bodies. ... We might very well say that an audience does not see with its eyes but with its lungs, does not hear with its ears but with its skin. (p. 150)

As I shall show, the notion that performance might be communicating with its audiences by a mysterious form of osmosis was the source of considerable anxiety in the past. But today many practitioners and scholars consider the bodily engagement of audiences to be something to explore, exploit, and celebrate.

For example, a collection of essays edited by Sally Banes and André Lepecki, *The Senses in Performance* (2006), analyses subtle and creative uses of smell, touch, and taste in performance, as well as sight and hearing. Far from directing us back to the body as a universal common denominator, this collection provides a useful reminder that 'modes of attention' are subject to change over time as developments in technology provide us with new forms of perception (p. 4). It also reflects the profound influence of phenomenological philosophy and the work of Maurice Merleau-Ponty. In *The Phenomenology of Perception* (1945), Merleau-Ponty reminds us that our entire experience of the world is embodied and that this embodiment frames our every perception and thought. His insights arrived as a common point of reference in theatre and performance studies in the 1980s and 1990s, and they have been used to frame and legitimise scholarly discussion of corporeal responses: the 'gut reactions' that are integral to the experience of theatre-going.

Despite the growth in academic interest in embodied experience, some aspects of corporeal response and behaviour commonly shared by theatre-goers remain little explored. Baz Kershaw's discussion of the phenomenon of applause in

'Oh! For Unruly Audiences! Or, Patterns of Participation in Twentieth-Century Theatre' (2001) examines one of these aspects. Kershaw contemplates the changing behaviour that has surrounded the convention of applause and speculates about why theatre scholars have not engaged with the subject, despite its ubiquity as part of the contemporary experience of theatre-going:

> Perhaps theatre analysts do not want to acknowledge applause in the context of serious scholarship because it is perceived to be incidental to performance. Or perhaps applause ... is in itself a thoughtless act, maybe a response arising from a basic impulse or reflex action, over which, in the end, we have no control. ... we seem to be too mystified or even ashamed by the way we have acquired the habit [of applause] to want to talk about it openly. (pp. 134–5)

Kershaw proposes that the shame that surrounds applause is related to a sense of being compromised by participation in a collective expression of approval or to a sense of discomfort at being caught up in a ritual which, ultimately, 'fits us out for hegemonic submission' (pp. 134–5).

Since the publication of Kershaw's article, other commentators have observed that there is something strange going on in these moments at the end of a show. Writing in *Stage Fright, Animals and Other Theatrical Problems* (2006), Nicholas Ridout bears witness to this 'unease, the sense that this is not quite right' (p. 164), and proposes that its source lies in an attempt to obscure the economic basis of the theatrical event. He suggests that the audience's proffering of thanks for something they have already paid for is indicative of a curious collective fantasy about the nature of the exchange, observing: 'The audience is trying to figure itself as the recipient of a gift' (p. 165). For Ridout, the ritual of applause contains an awkward reminder of the audience's complicity in – but simultaneous disavowal of – the hegemony of consumerism in our capitalist culture.

This awkwardness is, of course, intensified at the end of a show which has presented its audience with particularly challenging or disturbing material. British actor Simon Callow (probably best known for his appearance as the Scottish bon viveur Gareth in the 1994 film *Four Weddings and a Funeral*) reveals that performers also feel the discomfort that Kershaw and Ridout describe. He recalls performing in David Hare's play about land reform in communist China, *Fanshen*, with the theatre company Joint Stock in the 1970s. He notes: 'It seemed inappropriate, after thus throwing down the gauntlet, to come on to our hopefully chastened bourgeois audience all beams and bashfulness' ('Darling, We Were Wonderful!', *The Guardian*, 16 June 2008). Callow's account of the cast's ultimately fruitless attempts to find an appropriate way of dealing with the curtain call reveals the problems inherent in producing ostensibly radical, political performance within the framework of the theatre establishment. It also reflects the difficulty of negotiating the swift transition in the relationship between audience and actor as the latter leaves the stage 'in character' and then returns a moment later to deliver a final performance – supposedly without artifice – where the appearance of genuine, if formal, acknowledgement of thanks is the norm.

What should be becoming clear is that there are a vast range of methodological approaches to audiences in theatre studies. At one end of the spectrum it is possible to find historical studies of audience which adopt an empirical, materialist approach. These are effectively exemplified by Jim Davis and Victor Emeljanow's *Reflecting the Audience* (2001), a tightly focused historical account of London theatre-going between 1840 and 1880. The book draws upon archival material and uses statistical analysis to construct a precise cultural geography of place and period, and it offers extraordinarily detailed information on such things as train timetables and the cost of tickets and travel. At the other end of the spectrum are writers whose work is informed by developments in critical theory, including poststructuralist thought and psychoanalysis. For example, Anne Ubersfeld's 'The Pleasure of the Spectator' (1982), drawn from *L'École du spectateur* (1981), explores both the pleasures afforded by theatre and what it denies its audiences. Ubersfeld uses Freudian theories which propose that the formation of identity in childhood is predicated upon the condition of unfulfillable desire, and she links this to the limits of the pleasures available to the spectator in the theatre, arguing that both the ephemerality of the theatrical experience and the volatility of the spectator's desire mean that the relationship between the two will be one of permanent frustration. She observes that

> the object flees from the eye and the touch of the
> one that desires it: not only the actor flees from
> us, but all the beauty shimmering on the surface
> of the stage. ... And the flight of our desire is no
> less frustrating than the flight of the object: the
> desire of the spectator travels from object to
> object. (p. 138)

Herbert Blau's *The Audience* (1990) also positions performance as the site of desire and displacement. Blau presents the audience 'not so much as a mere congregation of people as a body of thought and desire' (p. 25) and focuses upon questions of repression, asking why we return again and again to view disturbing, upsetting spectacles of violence and pain that we can hardly bear to watch.

Blau's and Ubersfeld's interest in psychoanalytic theory and individual response fed into the emergence and development in the 1990s of performance analysis which draws upon the affective and emotional experience of the writer. This approach is sometimes described as 'performative writing' and is well represented in Peggy Phelan's 'On Seeing the Invisible: Marina Abramović's "The House with the Ocean View"' (2004). This piece intertwines conventional academic analysis of the social and artistic context of Abramović's work with letters – ostensibly from Phelan to Abramović – which detail Phelan's relationship to Abramović's work, Phelan's personal history, and her physical and emotional responses to 'The House with the Ocean View' (Sean Kelly Gallery, New York, 2002).

At its best this approach can show how fully our responses to performance are generated by individual preoccupations and experiences, as well as allowing the writer to explore – and thus validate – emotional and physiological aspects of response which will never be captured by statistical analysis and which have not been considered 'proper' subjects for academic analysis in the past. Phelan discusses her physical discomfort, her tears, and her embarrassment, for example. She describes the moment when she meets Abramović's gaze during the eighth day of the twelve-day durational piece in which Abramović lived in a raised space without eating, speaking, reading, or writing, in full view of the people passing through the gallery:

> I was taken aback by the intensity, the density of your eyes. ... Before long, I was sweating. You slowly came off the wall and began to walk towards me. As you walked, my body began to shake. My left buttock began to tremble. I became extremely self-conscious. The gallery was crowded and I was worried that everyone was staring at my one jiggling buttock. But you kept coming closer, and the closer you came the more I shook. (p. 24)

Phelan's writing demonstrates that analysis of performance can be a creative act in and of itself. It also highlights an individual experience of spectatorship, rather than mass audience response, and provides a valuable reminder that emotional and embodied responses have a significant and legitimate role in the analysis of performance. In less capable hands than Phelan's, however, this approach can open itself to accusations that it fails to situate the performance within a broader social context, that it replaces rigorous research with self-indulgent soul-searching, and that it ultimately tells us more about the writer than about the work being commented upon.

The vast methodological gap between Phelan's exploration of affect and the empirical approach pursued by scholars such as Davis and Emeljanow makes the wide range of methodological approaches to the study of audiences within theatre studies starkly apparent. But common to scholars across the discipline is interest in one figure: the active audience member. Bennett, for example, is upfront about the fact that the 'productive and emancipated spectator' is central to *Theatre Audiences* (p. 1). She presents her readers with a brief historical account of the gradual pacification of audiences – moving from a high point of active engagement in the religious festivals of ancient Greece to the complete separation between stage and darkened auditorium realised in the naturalist theatre of Paris and Moscow at the end of the nineteenth century. The heart-felt opening phrase in the title of Baz Kershaw's 'Oh! For Unruly Audiences!' is also telling. Most theatre scholars prefer their audiences actively engaged.

This preference has had a significant impact upon our understanding of theatre's histories. Indeed, the enthusiasm for stories of riots and disturbance in the theatre can sometimes give the impression that audiences of old did little *but* riot. The attraction for theatre enthusiasts is obvious: theatre riots suggest a bygone age when theatre was a venue for genuine public debate and dialogue where audiences could express themselves without inhibition and effect social change. As a result theatre buffs tend to recall them with affection and some nostalgia. In fact, the creativity of certain rioters has even encouraged some historians to consider riots to be performances in their own right. Neil Blackadder's *Performing Opposition: Modern Theater and the Scandalized Audience* (2003) covers the premiere of Gerhardt Hauptmann's *Before Sunrise* at Berlin's Freie Bühne in 1889, Parisian audiences' first encounters with Alfred Jarry's *Ubu Roi* in 1896, the protests in Dublin which greeted J. M. Synge's *Playboy of the Western World* in 1906 and Sean O'Casey's *The Plough and the Stars* in 1926, and finally the response to Brecht's plays in Germany between 1922 and 1932. Blackadder's preface has much to tell us about the underlying beliefs fuelling interest in unruly audiences, as he begins with a quotation from a review of the disorderly premiere of Brecht and Kurt Weill's *The Rise and Fall of the City of Mahagonny* at the Leipzig Opera House in 1930. The reviewer, Alfred Polgar, observed: 'Theater scandals are tremendously stimulating. It's good to see people ready to come to blows over the theoretical questions which art brings up – or throws down – and getting so worked up that they're beside themselves' (p. ix). Blackadder admits his own interest in riots is generated by a similar response and acknowledges that he, like many other theatre scholars and practitioners, is deeply sympathetic to the director Artaud's desire to reach audiences on the deepest physical and emotional levels – to create 'a theatre that would be like a shock treatment, galvanise, shock people into feeling' (p. xvi).

I will return to this preference for theatre which shocks and stimulates to explore the other ideological biases and blind-spots it creates in theatre criticism. But, for now, this brief description of the analysis of reception of performance indicates the wide range of approaches in the field and the lack of consensus on methodology. I certainly think the current diversity of approaches in this field should be celebrated. What troubles me, though, is what is left out.

The road less travelled: asking the audience (rather than the reviewers)

One curious – and I think telling – omission is the low level of engagement with the theories and analytic approaches generated by cultural studies. This might seem surprising, given theatre studies' willingness to adopt and incorporate theories from the study of film and literature. Perhaps this omission is explained by a belief – voiced by Tracy C. Davis and Bruce McConachie in their introduction to a 1998 issue of *Theatre Survey* dedicated to audience research – that research in this area had long been dominated by a simplistic 'sender–message–receiver model' of communication which did not account for the possibility of unexpected or resistant responses on the part of audiences (p. 3). It is certainly true that early work in cultural studies often characterised the mass audience as vulnerable, passive, and malleable, taking a pessimistic view of popular entertainment. For example, *Dialectic of Enlightenment* (1973) – first published in 1944 by members of the Frankfurt School Theodor Adorno and Max Horkheimer – presented popular entertainment as a means of ensuring the integration of the individual into society by providing the ordering of free time. But since cultural studies' arrival as an academic discipline in the 1970s, it has crossed a broad terrain in pursuit of the audience. It has produced sophisticated and complex analyses of television, radio, film, advertising, video, popular music, the Internet, and literature in its broadest sense: magazines, comics, shopping catalogues, pornography, and wartime propaganda leaflets. Ultimately, cultural studies has come to be characterised by a rejection of the notion of 'the audience' as a singular or homogeneous entity, a detailed interrogation of diverse and sometimes unexpected responses, and an ethnographic engagement with the range of cultural conditions which inform an individual's viewing position: his or her class, gender, age, nationality, religious background, ethnicity, sexuality, geographical location, and education.

Theatre studies, however, has been slow to make use of theories from this field. Susan Bennett, for example, concludes her chapter in *Theatre Audiences* on 'Theories of Reading and Viewing' with the acknowledgement that she has chosen not to touch upon investigations into television audiences because

> [t]elevision, above all, lacks the sense of public event that attaches to both theatre and cinema. It denies the audience the sense of contact with the

> performers that is integral to any theatrical per-
> formance and, moreover, it denies the spectator-
> to-spectator communication ... within the larger
> framework of audience as community. (p. 84)

I will return to recent developments in performance that trouble Bennett's assumption that contact with performers and other spectators is a necessary part of theatrical perform-ance. Her lack of interest in the methods and approaches adopted by cultural studies scholars is indicative of a broader conceptual and ideological gap between the disciplines, which is most apparent in differences in methodology.

The most obvious of these differences is cultural studies' practice of observation and detailed questioning of audiences and consumers. This engagement with 'ordinary' mem-bers of the audience is notably absent from theatre studies. Whereas researchers working on television and film engage with audiences through surveys, in-depth interviews, and ethnographic research, almost no one in theatre studies seems to be interested in exploring what actual audience members make of a performance. Of course, there is now a whole side of the theatre industry which is professionally preoccupied with the thoughts, responses, and tastes of audi-ence members and which is dedicated to asking them what they think of the shows they have seen. While academic the-atre studies continues to engage with hypothetical models of spectatorship, statistical analysis of historical audiences, or the writer's personal experience, theatre marketing depart-ments are busy surveying the opinions and responses of real audiences through focus groups, interviews, and surveys, a development which Bennett comments upon in a 2006 article, 'Theatre Audiences, Redux'. As yet theatre studies has not mimicked this kind of engagement with audience, nor has it tried to make use of this kind of research, which is being produced regularly by individual theatre companies, arts funding organisations, and other organisations that Bennett lists, including the Society of London Theatres, the Broadway League (previously the League of American Theatres and Producers), and the Wallace Foundation (all of which provide reports on this research on their websites). This may be surprising, but academic scholarship and the theatre industry have very different motivations for their interest in audiences and pursue very different forms of inquiry as a result. Theatre scholars are, for the most part, interested in how audiences interpret what they have seen, whereas the industry is concerned with ensuring the profitability of its investment and is consequently more interested in why a production appeals and in generalising about patterns of consumption. These differences are highlighted in Christopher Olsen's 2002 assessment of the surveys being used by a range of professional theatres in North America, 'Theatre Audience Surveys: Towards a Semiotic Approach'. Olsen found that these surveys commonly focus upon establishing quantifiable demographic information, such as the age, income, and occupation of patrons, and rarely include questions which address the content of productions or qualitative issues.

Nevertheless, there are indications that the theatre industry is attempting to develop a more nuanced understanding of audiences. Interviews with programmers, curators, and artistic directors collected in Thomas Frank and Mark Waugh's *We Love You: On Audiences* (2005) reveal that some arts festivals and venues now go to extraordinary lengths to find out more about the preferences and lifestyles of their audiences. Mark Ball, artistic director of the annual Birmingham performing arts festival Fierce!, describes the focus groups and extensive telephone surveys organised by an external marketing agency commissioned by the festival. These go much further than establishing how audience members found out about the show in the first place. They allow consideration of the experience of a show in the context of a whole night out: where else audience members might go and whom they are spending the evening with. As Ball puts it, the aim is to 'get under the skin of audiences, to try and understand who they are and why they come. To know what their motivations are' (p. 102).

There are also some signs that theatre studies is beginning to engage with the industry's approach to audiences. For example, John Tulloch's *Shakespeare and Chekhov in Production and Reception: Theatrical Events and Their Audiences* (2005) uses quantitative data, focus group discussions, and case studies of selected audience members as well as detailed qualitative surveys and interviews. Tulloch also employs the media studies concept of 'audiencing' to address how the cultural frames of education, marketing, and criticism inform responses to productions of Chekhov and

Shakespeare. The theory of 'audiencing' proposes that audiences are constructed by institutions, discourses, and interpretive frames. As Pertti Alasuutari argues in *Rethinking the Media Audience* (1999), it encourages us to think of the audience as 'a discursive construct produced by a particular analytic gaze' (p. 6). Using this approach in an earlier article, 'Approaching Theatre Audiences: Active School Students and Commoditised High Culture' (2000), Tulloch explores how education programmes in theatres function to attract and maintain audiences. He discusses the Royal Shakespeare Company's policy of running seminars for school parties, concluding that these not only are intended to 'capture future adult subscribers early' but that they are 'also designed to reproduce at least one mass audience per season, with plenty of school "bums on seats"'. Ultimately, he claims, '"Audiencing" of school students is...a highly regulated marketing exercise in many countries' (pp. 88–9). But Tulloch does not leave it there. His interviews with school students reveal that they are far from passive in their response to these high-cultural texts, as they bring their own experiences to the interpretation of the productions, generating readings which differ significantly from those of their teachers. Similarly, Matthew Reason's research into Scottish school pupils' memories of a live theatre event, which is reported in a two-part article titled 'Young Audiences and Live Theatre' (2006), reveals that their responses are profoundly influenced by their previous experience of theatregoing. The work of Tulloch and Reason indicates the value of asking audience members what they make of the theatre they see. It demonstrates the diversity of response to theatre events among audiences and provides insights into the perspective of an age group which is unrepresented among academics and professional reviewers.

Nevertheless, in adopting this investigative approach, Tulloch and Reason remain in a small minority among theatre studies scholars. I am not the only person to have noticed this. In *Reading the Material Theatre* (2004), Ric Knowles argues, 'Precisely how audiences produce meaning in negotiation with the particular, local theatrical event, fully contextualised … has only rarely been analysed or modelled in any detail' (p. 17). He claims that this is what he is going to do, but his analysis of touring productions concentrates on performances that he has seen himself and 'draws heavily upon local reviews' (p. 21). He explains that these reviews should not be read as 'evidence of what audiences-in-general felt and understood – and therefore what the performance "really meant" – but as evidence of meanings and responses that specific performances in particular locations made available' (p. 21). This is fair enough. But Knowles's fascinating, and otherwise exemplary, study neatly elides the continuing absence of the voices and opinions of 'ordinary' audience members who have no professional links to the theatre, and it reflects the broader scholarly tendency to focus upon the response of published reviewers.

The problems of relying upon the responses of reviewers are manifold. For a start, British theatre reviewers can in no way be described as representative of 'audiences-in-general', as was made clear by the heated controversy sparked by off-the-cuff remarks made in the press in 2007 by National Theatre director Nicholas Hytner. Hytner's comments were elicited in an interview in which he was asked to speculate on the prejudices that prominent female theatre directors have had to overcome. He argued that 'too many of the theatre critics are dead white men' ('Dead White Men in the Critic's Chair Scorning the Work of Women Directors', *The Times*, 14 May 2007). Unsurprisingly, these remarks were roundly rejected by the reviewers, not least for their implicit ageism. Michael Billington asserted that the critic should not be required to be representative of the audience: 'We are not there as audience representatives or spokespersons. We are there to describe, analyse and evaluate what we see. We may be right or wrong, according to taste, but we are individuals expressing an opinion rather than tribunes of the people' ('My Showdown with Nick Hytner', *The Guardian*, 24 May 2007). Hytner decided to qualify his remarks in the press two weeks later in response to these objections. He acknowledged the value of the kind of critical expertise acquired over decades of theatre-going but argued that theatre reviewers might benefit from a more varied cultural diet. He also insisted – quite correctly – that 'the first-string critics of all the major daily papers ... are male, white, over 50, and Oxbridge-educated' ('Dear Critics: Why Not See a Film for a Change?', *The Observer*, 3 June 2007).

Concerns about the insularity and parochialism of the British critical establishment are not new. Kalina Stefanova's series of interviews with London theatre reviewers and influential theatre practitioners, collected in *Who Keeps the*

Score on the London Stages? (2000), records similar sentiments. Richard Eyre – director of the National Theatre between 1987 and 1997 – described the critical world as 'a closed circle'; well-known playwright, actor, and director Steven Berkoff (not known for his love of critics, as we shall see) stated it remained 'too dull in its tastes'; and David Farr (director of the Gate, 1995–1998, and the Lyric Hammersmith, 2005–2008) argued that the tendency to refer to previous productions in reviews of Shakespeare is 'negative in terms of its introspection' (pp. 56–7). Clearly, for practitioners – and for audience members who may imagine that reviewers' long experience of theatre-going lends their judgements special cultural authority – the question of taste does matter. Surely it is the responsibility of critics to keep their reviews – or of newspapers to keep their reviewers – abreast of changing cultural tastes and trends? Without such awareness – and a willingness to look to the future as well as celebrate the past – the critical commentary on performance appearing in the daily press can only become an increasingly obstructive and anachronistic drag upon new developments in theatre and performance.

But perhaps it is inevitable that the experience of the theatre critic differs vastly from that of the rest of the audience. Theatre-going is not an occasional – and often hugely expensive – treat for these writers: it is a professional necessity. And although their expertise qualifies them for the job, it ensures that they have little in common with the majority of theatre-goers. They might, for example, be able to compare the approach of the latest interpretation of *Hamlet* with those of the past five productions they have seen, but the pleasure of watching a classic play to see how it ends is going to be a distant memory for them. It is also important to remember that theatre reviews are written to entertain, are allotted limited space on the printed page, and are produced under tight deadlines. Stefanova's interviews indicate that reviewers are aware of these problems. Some reviewers admit that the critic can experience theatre 'fatigue' or a loss of perspective; others acknowledge that the speed at which a review is composed leaves little time to reflect upon response, leading in some cases to a superficial judgement which the critic may come to regret. Some also reflect upon their relationship with the industry, suggesting that the growth in preview features – which provide a show with publicity without passing judgement on its content – may compromise the position of the critic. The question of the role and function of contemporary theatre criticism requires more space than I am able to give it here. But this short discussion does, I hope, make apparent the problems of using reviews as a measure of audience response.

An obvious question remains. Theatre scholars cannot be unaware of these problems with reviews, so why do they continue to cite them? When dealing with theatre history, the answer is obvious: the written record – in the form of reviews – may be all that remains of the audience's reaction. In the case of contemporary performance, it may be a matter of disciplinary allegiance. As Christopher Balme rightly points out in *The Cambridge Introduction to Theatre Studies* (2008), the majority of theatre scholars are not trained in the fields of empirical psychology and sociology, and in consequence the delivery of rigorous audience research presents them with substantial methodological challenges (p. 34). Moreover, there is little incentive for these researchers to invest the time and energy required to master the skills required to investigate audience response fully while their colleagues remain primarily preoccupied with the production of performance rather than its reception.

It seems important to ask whether residual cultural attitudes towards 'ordinary' audience members are informing these methodological choices. An assessment from outside the discipline of theatre studies' attitudes towards audiences may prove useful here. In his 2004 review of Susan Kattwinkel's collection *Audience Participation: Essays on Inclusion and Performance* (2003), film and television expert Martin Barker finds among its essays evidence of enduring suspicion of popular entertainment, as well as attitudes towards audiences which are reminiscent of Adorno and Horkheimer's dismissive pessimism. He notes the collection's failure to address questions of pleasure and detects an 'implied damnation of "traditional theatre"' in its promotion of the radical energy of performance. He observes that 'the implicit model is pure, unconsidered Frankfurtism'. If Barker is right, perhaps a residual distrust of the mass and a lack of respect for the intellectual and interpretive capacities of 'ordinary' theatre-goers might explain why scholars continue to cite the opinions and reactions of published reviewers rather than asking audience members what they think. But I would argue that this suspicion of the mass audience

– if this is what it is – is not simply an inheritance of early twentieth-century concerns about the deleterious influence of the mass media. It is being sustained by twenty- first-century fears about the ignorance and malevolence that may be contained within the anonymous populace, and it also has roots which lie buried deep among much longer-lived cultural anxieties.

Suspicion, frustration, and contempt: attitudes towards audiences

Certainly, the powerful emotions that the contemplation of theatre audiences appears to generate may provide us with one explanation for this apparent aversion to asking audience members what they make of the performances they attend. And suspicion of the effects of the seductive, hypnotic power of mimesis – the copying of reality frequently practised in theatre – can be traced back a long way. Jonas Barish's *The Antitheatrical Prejudice* (1981) is a weighty tome that details several centuries' worth of this distrust. Barish has a great deal of material to work with: European history is littered with examples of this prejudice. He starts in ancient Greece with the philosopher Plato, who famously planned the exclusion of poets and theatre from his ideal city-state, the Republic. Plato's hostility to the theatre is grounded in his aversion to copies and imitations, which he considers impure, distorted, and debased. For Plato, mimesis is an anarchic force which appeals to the passions. It is difficult to overstate the strength of his aversion. As Barish observes, for Plato, 'Mimesis, which can place new and unsettling

thoughts in the mind, must be treated as a dangerous
sive. ... It works chiefly on the irrational side of us,
licence to our dreams and foul thoughts, to whatever
is devious, intricate, and disordering' (p. 26).

Theatre is singled out for censure in Plato's so
because it can be considered the quintessentially mir
art. As Barish points out, acting depends upon the a
tion and imitation of a range of roles and thus prese
challenge to the smooth functioning of the Republic, w
relies upon each citizen's adoption of a single, unchan
identity. So Plato's hatred of the theatre is based upon
anxiety that subjectivity and identity are destabilised
exposure to the unending alterity of the role-play presented
in the theatre. Indeed, it seems Plato believes that mimesis
even poses a threat to sanity. Barish claims – making reference to the incestuous relationship central to Sophocles'
Oedipus Rex – that for Plato '[i]t is nearly as terrible to imagine that one has married one's mother as it would be to do
so in earnest. The first can lead to the second and must be
prohibited' (p. 29). When one reads Plato's work, it can
seem as though theatre was responsible for all the crimes
and corruptions of his day.

Barish examines the reappearance of anti-theatrical prejudice throughout history. He explores the reasons for the
low status and persecution of actors in Roman times and the
emergence of early Christian preachers, such as Tertullian
and St Augustine, who saw the popular theatrical spectacles
of Rome as part of a wider diabolic conspiracy to enslave
human souls and rejected them for their idolatry, their

basis in pagan worship, and their association with pleasure. Opposition to the theatre generated a deluge of pamphlets and other publications in fifteenth-century Britain written by Puritans who saw play-going as a sin in and of itself. These publications include Jeremy Collier's *Short View of the Immorality and Profaneness of the English Stage* (1698) and the extraordinary *Histriomastix* (1633), in which William Prynne denounces theatre-goers as

> *Adulterers, Adulteresses, Whore-masters, Whores, Bawdes, Panders, Ruffians, Roarers, Drunkards, Prodigals, Cheaters, idle, infamous, base, prophane, and godlesse persons, who hate all grace, all goodnesse, and make a mocke of piety.* (quoted in Barish, pp. 86–7; his emphasis)

Prynne's hysterical attack does a good job of illustrating what Barish calls the 'unmistakably crackpot streak' (p. 2) that runs through many manifestations of anti-theatrical prejudice, but some of its proponents are philosophers who still command respect today, including the French philosopher Jean-Jacques Rousseau, whose *Letter to d'Alembert concerning Spectacles* (1758) vigorously attacked a proposal for a public theatre in Geneva.

Barish focuses upon the aspects of anti-theatrical prejudice which recur over time, arguing that its appearance in such diverse historical and geographical locations means that we should not look principally to social factors or economic conditions to explain it. He argues that the theatre evokes universally held and deeply rooted fears of 'impurity, of contamination, of "mixture", of the blurring of strict boundaries' (p. 87) which transcend differences of culture and that it evokes an 'ontological queasiness' (p. 3) in all of us. Barish's ahistoricism seems dated today, and a reassessment of the material he covers could usefully look at the differences among the philosophical, religious, and moral motivations underlying distinct instances of anti-theatrical prejudice. Nevertheless, there is no denying that various detractors have returned time and again to the negative effect that the theatre has upon those who witness it. It is also clear that these fears are not merely a historical phenomenon. In Britain they found form in the extraordinary system of theatrical censorship which lasted until 1968. An anti-theatrical animus can certainly be detected in the conclusion of the 1909 report of the British Joint Select Committee on Censorship and Licensing, which contrasts the threatening volatility of theatre to the decorous stability of the text:

> Ideas or situations which, when described on a printed page may work little mischief, when represented through the human personality of actors may have more power and a more deleterious effect. The existence of an audience, moved by the same emotions, its members conscious of one another's presence, intensifies the influence of what is done and spoken on stage. ... The

> performance, day after day, in the presence of
> numbers of people, of plays containing [inde-
> cency, libel and blasphemy] would have cumula-
> tive effects to which the conveyance of similar
> ideas by print offers no analogy. (*Report from the
> Joint Select Committee*, p. 188)

The committee's conclusions reflect an apparently ineradi-
cable obsession with the arousal of the audience through the
immorality of theatrical display.

Of course, suspicion of the audience has not always been
the preserve of the censorious enemies of freedom of theatrical expression. Many theatre practitioners have a profoundly
ambivalent relationship with audiences. This ambivalence
is most evident in the understandably conflicted relationship between performers and professional spectators – the
reviewers who sit in the auditorium, pen in hand, ready
to pass judgement in print. These tensions are particularly
apparent when they bubble over into a public spat. Here
good examples live on in anecdote: the evening in 1976 that
playwright David Storey laid into Michael Billington in the
bar at the Royal Court (detailed by Jasper Rees in 'The Day
David Storey Walloped a Critic', *The Daily Telegraph*, 9 July
2007); Steven Berkoff's threat to kill reviewer Nicholas de
Jongh after an uncomplimentary review of his Hamlet in
1979 (which Berkoff discusses in his autobiography, *Free
Association*, p. 59); John Osborne's efforts to set up what
he called the British Playwrights' Mafia, which would take
its revenge on uncomplimentary critics (described by David

Nathan in 'Playwrights' Mafia Declared War on Critics', *The Independent*, 27 December 1994).

The phenomenon of stage fright, however, suggests that there is something more complex going on than fear of a bad review, and here Ridout's examination of the problem in *Stage Fright, Animals, and Other Theatrical Problems* is very useful. Ridout provides an insightful account of the anxieties experienced by the actor upon exposure to an audience and discusses various methods employed to deal with this debilitating fear. He touches upon Stanislavski's techniques, which encourage actors to develop a disregard for the audience's presence, creating the experience of 'Solitude in Public'. For example, in *An Actor Prepares* the experienced director Tortsov tells the novice actor Kostya: 'You are in public because we are all here. It is solitude because you are divided from us by a small circle of attention. During a performance, before an audience of thousands, you can always enclose yourself in this circle like a snail in its shell' (p. 82, quoted in Ridout, *Stage Fright*, p. 39).

Ridout demonstrates how Stanislavski presents the experience of stage fright as central to the realisation of successful acting. He also proposes that stage fright is a specifically modern phenomenon, bound up with the development of psychoanalysis and theatrical naturalism, as well as the use of electric light in the theatre and the pressures of modern urban life. He argues that the industrialisation of entertainment, the actor's financial dependence upon a mass audience, and the audience's dependence upon the performance's punctual delivery are particularly problematic. These pressures come together in a quotation selected by Ridout from Henry James's novel *The Tragic Muse* (1890), in which the character Gabriel Nash complains that dramatists can hardly be expected to make serious art now that they are obliged to make concessions to 'the essentially brutal nature of the modern audience', who need 'to catch the suburban trains, which stop at 11.30'. Nash excoriates

> the omnium gatherum of the population of a big commercial city at the hour of the day when their taste is at its lowest, flocking out of hideous hotels and restaurants, gorged with food, stultified with buying and selling and with all the other sordid preoccupations of the age, squeezing together in a sweltering mass, disappointed in their seats — all before eleven o'clock! (pp. 66–7, quoted in Ridout, *Stage Fright*, p. 43)

Nevertheless, not all practitioners are ready to accept that a difficult and bruising encounter with an ungrateful audience is necessary. Some have concluded that the only solution to the audience's shortcomings is to remove their work from the public sphere. W. B. Yeats, for example, decried the popular, public theatre and declared his interest in an 'aristocratic' theatre for a small, select audience. He announced in 'A People's Theatre: A Letter to Lady Gregory': 'I want to create for myself an unpopular theatre and an audience like a secret society where admission is by favour and never to many' (*Explorations*, 1962, p. 335).

Some writers went much further. The closet dramas of Gertrude Stein, such as *Not Slightly* (1914) and *Counting Her Dresses* (1917), were designed for private contemplation by the reader rather than public viewing. In *Stage Fright: Modernism, Anti-Theatricality, and Drama* (2002) Martin Puchner demonstrates that Stein's preference for writing closet drama was the product of her belief that the experience of watching theatre involves constant and unhelpful interruptions which militate against emotional absorption in the work. For Puchner, Stein's attitude is representative of the modernist 'consecration' of the artwork and of a deep ambivalence about 'the masses'. He concludes that the fact that the making and watching of theatre inevitably involves collaborative and collective experience means that the theatre is 'anathema to many modernists', who sought to celebrate the individual's focused engagement with the autonomous artwork (p. 103). But Puchner also argues that the modernists' approach to theatre is not simply about privileging and enabling absorption. He makes the link between this attitude and a conservative political stance, as he claims that it was a response 'to the fear that the theatre would actually provide a forum in which the constitution of public opinion might take place' and that, ultimately, 'modernist anti-theatricalism attacked the theatre to foreclose direct political engagement' (p. 11).

Fortunately, withdrawal from the public sphere is not the only response to frustration with existing audiences. Dissatisfaction with audience response and behaviour often generates innovation and experiment in the theatre, and the desire to provoke, shock, and unsettle spectators is central to the avant-garde. Alfred Jarry, for example, seems to have been pleased with the scandal created by his play *Ubu Roi* (1896), which tracks the rise and fall from power of a fat, filthy, and corrupt buffoon, the eponymous Ubu. The play's cartoon-like violence, scatological language, and implausible action provoked outrage among Parisian audiences and generated pages of critical coverage in the press. Blackadder's full account of the scandal in *Performing Opposition* notes that Jarry kept a scrapbook of reviews which excluded the handful of positive notices the play received. This response was clearly linked to a deep contempt for the audience. Blackadder cites Jarry's opinion of the general public and its relationship to the theatre: 'It is because the public ... are an inert and obtuse and passive mass that they need to be shaken up from time to time so that we can tell from their bear-like grunts where they are – and where they stand' (p. 66). A similar antagonism was evident in the early twentieth-century Italian Futurist happenings inspired by manifestos such as Filippo Marinetti's 'The Pleasure of Being Booed', which envisages theatre as a 'martial art', a form of combat. These evenings strove to engineer confrontation, using tactics such as selling tickets for the same seat to ten people and putting glue on seats.

Bertolt Brecht is undoubtedly the best-known figure to have addressed the perceived passivity of theatre audiences, and the numerous techniques he adopted to try to create a critically engaged audience have become the stuff of theatre studies exam papers. The development of direct audience address, the use of episodic action, the inclusion of songs and film, and the ploy of leaving the lights up in the auditorium (to name just a few of Brecht's tactics) were all designed to encourage the audience to view social conditions which they had previously taken for granted in a new light, helping them understand that they could bring about social change. Brecht's efforts to create this *Verfremsdungeffekt* – or 'distancing effect' – were fuelled by a deep frustration with the passive audiences of the bourgeois theatre, which he called 'culinary theatre' because its audiences were like diners sating themselves with pleasure. His writings (collected in *Brecht on Theatre*, 2001) provide us with a series of vivid images and metaphors which illustrate his sense of the problems with his contemporary theatre and its audiences. Observing the behaviour of the audience in the theatre, he notes:

> They scarcely communicate with each other; their relations are those of a lot of sleepers. ... True, their eyes are open, but they stare rather than see, just as they listen rather than hear. They look at the stage as if in a trance. ... Seeing and hearing are activities, and can be pleasant ones, but these people seem relieved of activity and like men to whom something is being done.

Summing up, he observes that this theatre has transformed those watching 'into a cowed, credulous, hypnotized mass' (pp. 187–8).

Brecht makes it clear that he doesn't entirely blame the audience for this: these effects are produced in large part by the inadequacies of the contemporary theatre. But he does suggest that the audience bear a measure of responsibility for their plight. He notes that 'this audience hangs its brains up in the cloakroom along with its coat' (p. 27) and observes that audiences have a tendency to plunge into the illusion that they are watching an unrehearsed event which 'has to be checked' (p. 136). This disciplinarian tone and interest in the correction of what he views as inappropriate behaviour find expression elsewhere in his writing; he proposes that audiences will need training (p. 88) or a 'cold douche' (p. 132).

Occasionally, the frustrations of trying to get an appropriately engaged, politicised response, both from actors and from audiences, show through. Discussing the reception of his 1949 production of *Mother Courage* at the Deutsches Theatre in Berlin, Brecht acknowledges that audience members had not always responded to the play in the way he had hoped:

> From a number of press notices, however, and a
> lot of discussions with members of the audience
> it appeared that many people see Courage as
> the representative of the 'little people' who get
> 'caught up' in the war because 'there's noth-
> ing they can do about it', they are 'powerless in
> the hands of fate', etc. Deep-seated habits lead
> theatre audiences to pick on the characters'

more emotional utterances and forget all the rest.
(p. 220)

Sometimes it can seem as though Brecht's ideal – a critical, intellectually engaged, and questioning audience – is a long way from realisation.

Brecht's writings seem to be full of a genuine sorrow about the shortcomings of audiences, but this has not always been the mood among practitioners. Dan Rebellato's *1956 and All That* (1999) charts a shift in attitudes towards audiences in the British theatre establishment during the 1950s, from acceptance that audiences are, and should be, the 'ultimate arbiter of a performance's quality' to frustration with their failure to appreciate the work being presented to them (p. 107). He describes the way in which George Devine of the English Stage Company attempted to create a theatre at the Royal Court which was superior to the audience. He quotes John Osborne's memoirs, in which Osborne recalls Devine peering through the curtain at the punters on the first night of *The Entertainer*, urging, 'There you are, dear boy, take a look out there. ... What do you think of them, eh? Same old pack of cunts, fashionable arseholes. Just more of them than usual, that's all' (quoted in Rebellato, p. 112). Perhaps contempt for audiences is only likely to be expressed in such bald terms in memoirs and anecdotes, but it is clear that antagonism towards audiences did not abate in the 1960s.

In fact, Anne Wagner's description of several performances from the late 1960s and 1970s in her 2000 essay 'Performance, Video, and the Rhetoric of Presence' concludes that, in this period, 'the preoccupation with audience took on signally aggressive, even manic, desperate and coercive form' (p. 67). She describes a range of strategies to highlight the fact that the audience can be seen, including a number of performances which involved placing mirrors in front of the audience. Wagner's description of Dan Graham's *Performer/Audience/Mirror* (San Francisco Art Institute, 1975) leaves no doubt as to the painful self-consciousness these performances hoped to generate. Graham doubled the mirroring effect by standing at the front of the audience and providing a minutely detailed running commentary on their every cough and fidget. Wagner also discusses the work of performance artist Vito Acconci. In *Twelve Pictures* (The Theater, New York, 1969) Acconci strode across an unlit stage, taking photos of the audience as he went; in *Performance Test* (Emanu-El YM-YWHA, New York, 1969) Acconci simply stared at individuals in the audience for approximately thirty seconds. Acconci's unadorned description of the piece describes the effect: 'Audience looks at performance, performance looks back at it – the gaze of the audience results in nothing, is turned back on itself' (quoted in Wagner, pp. 72–3).

The confrontational stare, where performers, out of character, stand and silently watch an audience, has now become a recognisable theatrical trope. In *Devising Performance* (2006), Deirdre Heddon and Jane Milling comment on the regular use of this look, proposing that these moments serve to focus attention upon the audience's act of watching as performers mimic the behaviour of specta-tors. Heddon and Milling cite several performances which started and concluded with moments of mutual observa-tion, including the Living Theatre's *Mysteries and Smaller Pieces* (The American Centre for Students and Artists, Paris, 1964), in which the duration of a single perform-er's opening encounter with the audience is reported to have grown from six minutes to half an hour as the show developed on tour. This moment of confrontation is drawn out to play length by Handke's *Offending the Audience* – cited above – which presents an extraordinarily direct and sustained performed analysis of the passivity of conven-tional audience behaviour. The play interrogates its audi-ence's expectations of theatre and their behaviour. Four casually dressed speakers, on an empty stage, make a series of observations about the role of the audience and the situ-ation. The lights are up in the auditorium throughout. Just in case there was any doubt about the required effect, the performers comment: 'You are being looked at. You are unprotected. You no longer have the advantage of looking from the shelter of darkness into the light' (p. 7). They continue: 'You are the subject matter. The focus is on you' (p. 9). Then, a few minutes later: 'Why, you are breath-ing. Why, you are salivating. Why, you are listening. Why, you are smelling. Why, you are swallowing. Why, you are blinking your eyelids. Why, you are belching. Why, you are sweating. Why, how terribly self-conscious you are' (p. 20). This is accompanied by statements which present a series of refusals of representation, empathy, identification, and shared experience and is polished off with a long wave of insults.

Forced Entertainment have been responsible for more recent attacks upon audience passivity. In *Certain Fragments* (1999) Tim Etchells describes the moment in *Showtime* (Alsager Arts Centre, Stoke-on-Trent, 1996), after performer Cathy Naden's long description of the details of the suicide she imagines for herself, when Terry O'Connor (dressed, in cardboard, as a tree) suddenly bursts out: 'What the fuck are you looking at? What the fuck is your problem? Fuck off! Voyeurs! There's a fucking line and you've just crossed it. Where's your human decency?' O'Connor continues in this vein for some time, and her tirade draws attention to the difficulty of predicting how images and stories of suffering which circulate in the media and entertainment industries will be received. Sometimes they may function to raise awareness, transforming spectators into actively engaged witnesses and increasing the likelihood of a remedy for instances of injustice, distress, or pain. At other times they may simply sate the undeniable public appetite for gore, sensation, and Schadenfreude. O'Connor accuses the audience of being in the latter camp, positioning them as voyeurs to encourage reflection upon whether we should be watching spectacles of suffering when there is no possibility of making a useful intervention.

Other practitioners position audiences as victims. The playwright Howard Barker, for example, claims that it is not he but the British theatre establishment that holds the audience in contempt. In *Arguments for a Theatre* (1998),

he avers that 'our major companies … [and] our best directors … think of an audience as something not to be trusted,
a semi-educated mass in need of protection' (p. 34). He
states that '[t]he audience has been treated as a child' by the
English theatre, which is 'in fear of our own audience, as
a poor teacher is afraid of the class' (p. 45). A poem written by Barker in 1991, 'On the sickness of the audience',
describes the results of this infantilisation:

> Audiences learn bad habits
> Viruses affect them in their nerves
> …
>
> The symptoms can be annotated
> *The myopia of thinking all things must be clear*
> *The tumescence caused by the appetite for*
>   *enlightenment*
> *The unhealthy craving for laughter*
> *The morbid horror of taking offence*
> *The apoplexy of having paid good money to see this*
> *The feverish ache for moral platitudes* (pp. 124–5)

Barker proposes a theatre which, in his terms, 'honours'
its audience by giving them responsibility for interpretation. He insists upon the importance of offering ambigu-
ity, rather than clarity, and producing an individual rather
than a collective or unified response. Barker acknowledges
that audiences are likely to experience disappointment and
that their relationship to this theatre is likely to be characterised by hostility and frustration. Nevertheless, he insists

that 'the audience always exists for the work. It is actively in search of it' (p. 136).

It seems that playwrights and directors are not alone in their frustration with audiences. For example, Frank and Waugh's *We Love You: On Audiences* records the frustration of artistic directors, programmers, and curators who complain freely about their audiences' lack of curiosity and sense of adventure. Christine Peters, a freelance theatre and dance curator working in Hanover and Stuttgart, observes:

> An audience doesn't like to see things twice, and an audience doesn't like other languages. It has big concentration problems ... [and] prefers to send text messages or sleep during a performance. It doesn't read the performance texts properly beforehand and therefore asks stupid questions afterwards. It doesn't like to see unknown artists. It hates interactive performances, though when it experiences them, it is usually very excited afterwards. It talks about a lot of things it hasn't seen, but heard of. (p. 103)

Other programmers and curators also expressed irritation with a lack of curiosity among audiences, arguing that they tend to stick with what is familiar.

How to explain these expressions of frustration with, and contempt and downright hatred of, audiences issuing from the theatre? Some statements seem to be grounded in a fear of crowds or disdain for 'the masses' or to be generated by anger that those watching are not giving a carefully prepared performance the respect and attention it deserves. Others seem to partake of the anti-theatrical belief that audiences are complicit in their seduction by performance's hypnotic power. But perhaps the single most powerful reason for these aggressive attacks is the continuing investment in the idea that theatre-going should be an improving and educational activity. For example, *We Love You* records Annemie Vanackere (theatre, dance, and youth theatre programmer at Rotterdam Schouwburg) giving revealing answers to her own rhetorical questions: 'The challenge is, I think, how can I make sure that people come to the things that I really think are important? There's also still something missionary about it. Why do we want people to come? ... we think it's good for you' (p. 105). Ultimately, it seems that the suspicion, contempt, and aggression directed towards audiences are a result of the belief that performance should somehow be 'good for you' and that 'you' might fail to recognise or appreciate that.

Potent orthodoxies: participation and empowerment

Many people still share Vanackere's faith in theatre's potential to be educative and empowering, to enable critical and ethical engagement, to awaken a sense of social responsibility, or to raise an audience's sense of its own political agency. What's more, many practitioners have decided to move beyond castigating audiences for their passivity towards enabling their active participation in performance.

This investment in audience participation is evident in many distinct fields, including community-based productions which place the emphasis upon the involvement of non-professionals, the learner-centred Theatre in Education movement, Augusto Boal's Forum Theatre, and the environmental theatre and performance art of the 1960s and later which invited or provoked audience intervention.

Of course, not all theatres or performance practices which foreground the role of the audience or create opportunities for audience interaction are accompanied by convenient mission statements setting out the ideological underpinnings of their investment in the concept of participation. But where practitioners do talk about the aim of such strategies, participation is often figured as a potent method of empowerment. This is certainly apparent in Boal's much-cited model of the spect-actor in Forum Theatre. The results are described in Boal's *Theatre of the Oppressed* (1979):

> [T]he spectator no longer delegates power to his
> characters either to think or to act in his place.
> The spectator frees himself; he thinks and acts for
> himself! Theater is action! Perhaps the theater is
> not revolutionary in itself; but have no doubts, it
> is a rehearsal for revolution. (p. 122)

Indeed, the belief that participation empowers has become a compelling orthodoxy in theatre and performance studies. And, like most orthodoxies, it often seems to be applied reductively and uncritically.

In some cases, this reductiveness seems to be a result of the writer's hope that vigorous affirmation will prove effective. Writing amid the potent revolutionary atmosphere in Paris in 1968, the French performance artist Jean-Jacques Lebel made the connection between creative and political agency explicit:

> No more theatre or expensive spectacles for a passive audience of consumers – but a truly collective enterprise in political and artistic research. A new type of relationship between the 'doers' and the 'lookers' is being experimented with. Perhaps we will succeed in helping hundreds of thousands more to let go of their alienated social roles, to be free of mental Stalinism, to become the political and creative doers they dream of being. (Quoted in Sandford, *Happenings and Other Acts*, 1995, p. 283)

The movement in this manifesto from confident assertion, through to acknowledgement that this 'new type of relationship' is still at the experimental stage, to Lebel's cautious 'Perhaps', indicates that it is written in hope rather than certainty, but similar hopes are still nurtured today.

A short essay by *Guardian* critic Lyn Gardner, written for the 2007 *Programme Notes* collection edited by Brine and Keidan, characterises the first years of the twenty-first century as being driven by the search for new relationships between performers and audiences. It argues that commentators and venues are lagging behind contemporary audiences' taste for the intimacy of live art. Gardner's article contains none of Lebel's caution. Gardner bears witness to audience members' desire to interact with performers, gradually building a sense of the urgency of this need throughout the piece. Her final image makes an explicit connection between artistic and political revolutions: 'The audiences are already storming the barricades, it is up to the rest of us to give them a helping hand because the revolution has already started without us, and it would be such a pity to miss it' (p. 16). Of course, Gardner's article is written to encourage and inspire venue programmers to take a chance on new forms of performance, and it would hardly be fair to accuse her of failing to provide her readership with evidence to support her contention that participation in performance 'allows us ownership of our own lives and own imaginative processes' (p. 13). But scholarly writing on the subject should surely be expected to substantiate its claims.

Kurt Lancaster's article 'When Spectators Become Performers and Theater Theory' (1997) contains claims which echo those made in Gardner's article. Lancaster focuses upon the interactive elements of a variety of 'performance-entertainments', including karaoke, role-playing games, tours of film industry theme parks in Florida, and theatre productions such as *Tony n' Tina's Wedding* (Washington Square Church and Carmelita's Restaurant, New York, 1988), which positions audience members as wedding guests. Lancaster uses Boal's theories to frame his analysis

of these cultural phenomena, proposing that 'these performances give people the opportunity to inject their own
values and beliefs into the event. As a result, participants
are able to break out of restrictive social roles: the role of
an over-worked laborer, mother, teen-ager, or student, for
example' (p. 77). Lancaster does not go on, however, to
demonstrate how this might be so. Here, Boal's cautionary
proviso that 'theater is not revolutionary in itself' appears to
have been forgotten. For Lancaster, the logic which equates
participation with empowerment seems self-evident, inex-
orable even; his article does not acknowledge that some of
its readers might question the link between singing along
to a karaoke machine and profound personal transformation or ask how, exactly, 'an over-worked laborer' might
use her visit to a film studio to make significant changes to
her life. Lancaster's sunny description of the pleasurable
productivity of participation does not begin to touch upon
the possible challenges to such transformations.

Lancaster was not the only person to make claims
for the political agency of participatory artwork in the
1990s. Nicolas Bourriaud's influential collection of essays
Esthétique rélationnelle (1998; *Relational Aesthetics*, 2002)
labelled and celebrated a novel trend in the contemporary
art world. Bourriaud described 'Relational Art' as the
creation of a social environment where people could participate in a shared activity and interact with each other
in art galleries; examples include hanging out on a ham-
mock, eating curries cooked by the artist, and dancing
to music provided on Walkmans (Gabriel Orozco, *Hamoc*

en la moma, MoMA, New York, 1993; Rirkrit Tiravanjia, *Untitled (Still)*, 303 Gallery, New York, 1992; Felix Gonzalez-Torres, *Untitled (Arena)*, Jennifer Flay Gallery, Paris, 1993). Bourriaud claimed that these forms of contemporary art were 'developing a political project' (p. 17), observing:

> What [these artists] produce are relational space-time elements, inter-human experiences trying to rid themselves of the straitjacket of the ideology of mass communications, in a way, of the places where alternative forms of sociability, critical models and moments of constructed conviviality are worked out. (p. 44)

Bourriaud has since been criticised for his failure to reflect upon the limitations of the artwork he describes. In an article titled 'Antagonism and Relational Aesthetics' (2004) Claire Bishop argues that the art that Bourriaud celebrates puts sociability where dissent and critique – the cornerstones of a democratic system based upon antagonistic debate – should be. She asserts: 'It is no longer enough to say that activating the viewer *tout court* is a democratic act'. She argues that the works described by Bourriaud risk collapsing into self-congratulatory entertainment for industry insiders. Bishop concludes that there is nothing intrinsically democratic about providing opportunities for convivial participation and that instead '[t]he tasks facing us today are to analyze *how* contemporary art addresses the viewer and to assess the *quality* of the audience relations it produces' (pp. 78–9; italics in the original).

Certainly, the confidence with which Bourriard and Lancaster move from descriptions of participatory activities to claims about political emancipation is in stark contrast to the approach adopted by many companies and academics working in Theatre in Education and with local communities, who often emphasise the continuing commitment, careful planning, and sensitivity required to realise the kind of positive transformation celebrated by Lancaster. Moreover, those who know most about this kind of work are very aware of its risks and cautious about making strong statements about its outcomes. In *Theatre, Education and the Making of Meanings* (2007) Anthony Jackson observes:

> Facile assumptions about being able to 'make a difference' in people's lives by the very act of engaging them in a participatory drama experience can all too easily lead to patronisation, even to a certain kind of oppression. ... There are perhaps few worse experiences in this field of work than to find oneself belittled or one's dignity undermined within a supposedly participatory event from which there is no ready escape. (p. 8)

As Jackson notes, complex emotions are aroused by participation in drama, and not all of them are positive.

Playing with the audience: uneasy interactions

The audience participation invited or engineered by performance art of the 1960s and later reveals that participation does not necessarily amount to empowerment. Most of the performances I describe below were darkly disturbing, were realised through manipulation or coercion, and sometimes provoked alarming responses from their audiences. Nevertheless, the unease and anxiety they played with may be considered central to their effect. For example, in the now-infamous *Rhythm 0* (Studio Morra, Naples, 1974) Marina Abramović placed herself at the mercy of her audience for six hours, having provided them with seventy-two objects, laid out on a table, to be used on her as they wished. These objects included an axe, a fork, perfume, a feather, chains, nails, a pen, and scissors. RoseLee Goldberg describes the results in 'Here and Now' (2000):

> As she stood passively beside the table, viewers turned her around, moved her limbs, stuck a thorny rose stem in her hand. By the third hour they had cut all her clothes from her body with razor blades and nicked bits of flesh from her neck. Later, someone put a loaded gun in her hand and pushed its nozzle against her head. (p. 246)

As Peggy Phelan points out, the audience participation enabled by this event was radically different from that offered in most performances. There was no unwritten script for the audience to follow, no clear actions to carry out, no roles proffered for adoption; there was simply a provocation. As a result, the audience became genuine co-creators of the performance. Phelan views this positively, arguing that the performance fulfils the 'promise of performance art', the 'possibility of mutual transformation during the enactment of the event' ('On Seeing the Invisible', p. 19). But the aggressive actions of some of those present make it hard to celebrate.

The problematic aspects of audience participation are also illuminated by the Living Theatre's controversial and iconic *Paradise Now!* (Avignon Festival, 1968). This production included direct audience address, one-to-one conversations and political debate, and the notorious 'Rite of Universal Intercourse', in which audience members took up the invitation to join nearly naked performers in a writhing 'love pile' on the stage – a scene which culminated in a chant of 'Fuck means peace'. The show generated censorious intervention from the authorities and theatre administrators, and critics accused the company of physically silencing vocal dissent from audience members and of being manipulative and oppressive in their efforts to shame spectators out of passivity. Even the directors acknowledged problems with the aggressive libidinous energy that was released by the production. Baz Kershaw discusses this production in *The Radical in Performance* (1999) and describes director Judith Malina's account of the sexual assault she endured during the scene while others in the group were immersed in their own pleasures around her. He concludes: 'The desire to completely free the spectator from spectatorship, at least in *Paradise Now!*, seems to have produced a theatrical pathology that played fast and loose with the virus of brute oppression' (p. 199).

The critical response to the 2005 London opening of the *Blue Man Group* (Astor Place Theatre, New York, 1991) indicates that concerns about the results of audience participation live on today. This slick, hi-tech mixture of mime, performance art, burlesque, tribal drumming, techno pop, and old-fashioned clowning grew out of experiments in performance art on the streets of New York and is now an enormous and hugely successful corporate enterprise with franchises in Toronto, Boston, Chicago, Berlin, and Las Vegas. Its audiences are primed for active involvement from the moment they enter the auditorium. Overhead digital message bars issue instructions on appropriate responses, ushers distribute strips of crêpe paper which audience members tie around their heads, and those seated in the front rows are given plastic ponchos to protect them from the paint and food which will fly later in the show. During the performance proper, audience members are invited up on stage: one endures a messy tea party; another is hoisted into the air upside down, doused in blue paint, and used as a human paintbrush, in an ironic homage to the work of artist Yves Klein. The eponymous blue men also leave the stage and crawl across the stalls, accompanied by live cameras which capture footage of audience members for giant screens on stage. They pin down an alarmed-looking audience member and appear to perform an impromptu gastric endoscopy using a fibre-optic camera.

The commercial success of the show indicates that these stunts clearly have a widespread appeal. But the model of participation the blue men exploit is one in which the complicity of audience members is assumed: they are coerced, rather than liberated; manipulated, rather than emancipated; instead of agency, they receive entrapment. As a result, critics who remain committed to the connection between audience participation and empowerment find the *Blue Man Group* difficult to stomach. Lyn Gardner's review of the show's London opening damned it as manipulative, vacuous, and sterile. Commenting on the audience participation, she observed: 'In some countries they call this torture; the Blue Man Group pass it off as entertainment' (*The Guardian*, 16 November 2005). Perhaps it is not surprising that the work of a global theatrical franchise creates this unease, but, then again, maybe Gardner is missing the point. Anxiety and apprehension are central to many of the effects and affects evoked by participatory performance.

This is certainly apparent in the large number of shows by young British theatre companies which use audience participation. For example, the large-scale installations organised by Punchdrunk are designed to test the audience's nerves. Hugely popular, these London productions, which have included *The Firebird Ball* (Offley Works, 2005), *Faust* (21 Wapping Lane, 2006), and *The Masque of the Red Death* (Battersea Arts Centre, 2007), extend the parameters of promenade performance. The company occupy and decorate entire buildings, and their shows frequently require audiences to move through a space rather than staying seated throughout. Instead of being led or directed from location to location, audience members wander through the venue at will, catching glimpses of performers and scenes as they happen across them. All audience members are required to wear white larval masks (which serve to distinguish them from the performers, hide their responses, and give them a ghostly anonymity); groups and couples who have come to the show together are encouraged to split up and explore the space separately; some spaces are dimly lit and occasionally completely dark.

Other companies give audiences a role to play or assign them a character as a group, playing upon the disquiet evoked by the uncertainty about exactly how much participation will be required. The London-based performance collective Shunt specialise in this technique, both teasing and terrifying their audiences. *The Ballad of Bobby François* (Arch 12a, Bethnal Green Railway Arches, 1999) positioned its audience as travellers on a flight which crashed; *Dance Bear Dance* (Arch 12a, Bethnal Green Railway Arches, 2002) figured audience members as delegates at a mysterious international convention where they were implicated in an incomprehensible plot to blow up a nameless common enemy; and *Amato Saltone* (London Bridge Vaults, 2006) initially positioned the audience as guests at a swingers party. Shunt's work proffers the pleasures of being 'an insider' while also provoking discomfort through the compromises such complicity can entail.

These techniques are not new. As Marco De Marinis points out in 'Dramaturgy of the Spectator' (1987), the director Jerzy Grotowski's early productions at the Theatre Laboratory in Opole, Poland, explored new spatial relationships between spectators and performers and gave the audience a group character. In *Faust* (1960) the audience were positioned as guests at Faust's table; in *Kordian* (1962) they were patients – or inmates – at a psychiatric clinic; in *Akropolis* (1962) they were figured as survivors of the gas chambers. These productions have clearly been influential, but Grotowski went on to reject this technique's coerciveness and took a decision in 1969 to move away from public performance towards what he termed 'paratheatre', which had no observers. As De Marinis reports: 'This somewhat constricting and basically authoritarian approach to audience participation [in Grotowski's earlier work] was later superseded and openly criticised by Grotowski, who saw it as counter-productive – rather than deconditioning the audience, this approach risked blocking and further inhibiting them' (p. 106).

Still, some of the companies responsible for today's most radical and creative experiments with audience participation seem very aware of its problems and deliberately work with them. This is certainly true of Blast Theory, another London-based group whose work puts participants centre stage, often placing them in situations that blur the boundaries between art and life, computer games and theatre. Their most notorious piece, *Kidnap* (undisclosed location, 1998), was advertised at cinemas in a forty-five-second video which included a freephone number for volunteers to call. Participants were selected via a lottery which gave the winners a chance to experience being kidnapped. The ten winners were put under surveillance before two of them were duly snatched and held in a secret location for forty-eight hours. Live webcasts made video of the events available to an online audience.

Another of the company's productions, *Uncle Roy All Around You* (ICA, London, 2003), made the participants into pawns in a three-dimensional computer game being played simultaneously on the Internet and on the streets of London's West End. After they arrived at the ICA, the live players exchanged their wallets, keys, and mobile phones for a tiny handheld computer, before being told to walk out onto the streets and follow the instructions and clues being sent to this device by the unseen Uncle Roy and the game's virtual participants, who were able to track the players' progress on the web. The aim of the game was to meet the eponymous Uncle Roy. When I played the game, I quickly became lost, following cryptic instructions which led me through the grid of pristine Georgian office blocks, leafy squares, and the busy Haymarket. Paranoia set in. I began to suspect anyone who passed me of being a stooge or another player, of being in on the game. Desperate to make the most of the hour allotted, I found myself running up and down the same streets, without being able to make sense of the instructions I was being given. One of my companions was luckier and made it to the conclusion of the game. He reached an office block where he was instructed to buzz for entry. After he had followed further clues to an office in the building, an interview via webcam followed. Once outside again, he had a ride in a limousine and was finally asked to commit to helping another player, should they request it, at any time during the next year.

Blast Theory's work challenges the conventional definition of an audience. In these pieces, the audience become performers; the city becomes the stage. They reconfigure the terms of the traditional theatrical encounter between participants and performers, as the artists who have designed and created the experience are often invisible, busy working behind the scenes. A live encounter between artist and audience may arrive belatedly, unexpectedly, or not at all, and the significance and value of 'spectator-to-spectator' contact – which is usually considered integral to any theatrical performance – is interrogated by moments such as the denouement of *Uncle Roy All Around You* (as 'successfully' experienced by my companion).

The experiences Blast Theory provides are illuminated by the work of Nicholas Abercrombie and Brian Longhurst, who reflect upon the changing nature of the modern audience in *Audiences: A Sociological Theory of Performance and Imagination* (1998). Abercrombie and Longhurst propose that recent developments in communications technology and the media environment mean that instead of thinking of audiences as 'dispersed' (watching a single television programme in separate locations) or 'simple' (watching a live event in a single location), we should now think of them as 'diffuse'. They observe that 'in contemporary society, everyone becomes an audience all the time. Being a member of an audience is no longer an exceptional event, nor even an everyday event. Rather it is constitutive of everyday life' (pp. 68–9). They argue that our engagement with diverse media is now so constant that performance has become ubiquitous: 'So deeply infused into everyday life is performance that we are unaware of it in ourselves or in others. Life is a constant performance; we are audience and performer at the same time; everybody is an audience all the time. Performance is not a discrete event' (p. 73).

Blast Theory's work certainly illustrates this effect, and I find it both thought-provoking and exciting. But there are connections to be made, I think, between their productions and the *Blue Man Group*. Although *Kidnap* and *Uncle Roy All Around You* foreground the role of the spectator, or the participant, they position her in a world where she is watched over by forces she cannot control, influence, or comprehend. *Kidnap* placed participants in a position of total passivity and submission; *Uncle Roy All Around You* presents its players with a game without telling them all the rules. In this game the player's complicity is taken for granted, and he is required to commit to helping another player without knowing what form that help might take or when he might be called upon to do so. The model of interaction presented is one in which freedom to choose is profoundly compromised by the limitations of the system in which choices are made. These shows' exploration of the limitations of interaction provokes in me a profound unease about the connections between participation and agency, both within the theatre and within the broader cultural and political sphere. Does the link between the two have substance, or is it merely an illusion?

It seems that this is the kind of concern that Blast Theory are hoping to provoke. Matt Adams, the company's artistic director, has acknowledged that there is always a danger of manipulation and glibness in participatory work and that many productions simply require participants to fit into roles that are already scripted for them. On the introductory page of the company's website, Adams points out that participation does not necessarily amount to empowerment, as he observes: 'These projects have posed important questions about the meaning of interaction and especially, its limitations. Who is invited to speak, under what conditions and what that is truly meaningful can be said?' (www.blasttheory.co.uk; accessed 27 March 2008). Adams goes further in a 2008 article for *Contemporary Theatre Review* (collectively authored by Adams, Steve Benford, and Gabriella Giannachi). He notes that the significant cultural shift towards interactivity and the inclusion of user-generated content 'both springs from and helps to further foster belief in the validity of the voice of the public within culture'. But he cautions that it is essential to consider the risks and tensions inherent in this move, as he asks:

> When does a consideration of the audience slide into a banal and redundant form of market provision? Does giving the public a voice within an artwork result in a collaborative work or merely

> provide pigeon holes for pre-scripted interven-
> tions? Is there any seriously democratic thread
> to this process or does the artist merely establish
> a benevolent dictatorship with him or her at the
> apex? (p. 227)

For Adams, these risks are clearly worth negotiating. He observes that participation in Blast Theory's pieces is designed to be disturbing and unsettling and that the 'game mechanic' central to most of their work ultimately encourages reflection upon '[t]he process of engaging with strangers and trying to find common cause with them' (p. 228). Adams makes no great claims for the transformative potential of these pieces, but the ethical impetus is there: they create imaginative spaces in which players can explore and assess their interactions with unknown ('ordinary') others in situations of unease, uncertainty, and anxiety.

Blast Theory's approach to their audiences seems refreshingly free of the sublimated anti-theatrical prejudice that appears to lurk behind much modernist theatrical experiment. The company seem to trust their audiences and give little – if any – sign that that they are frustrated with or suspicious of them. Other companies also seem ready to hand over responsibility to their audiences. Tim Etchells's comments in *Programme Notes* indicate the kind of thinking that now lies behind the experimentation of Forced Entertainment:

> I get excited by theatre and performance work
> that is brave enough to surrender control – trusting

its audience to think, trusting that they will go useful places when they're let off the leash of dramaturgical control, or even trusting that a trip through the ostensibly not so useful places (boredom, drifting, free-association) can be more than useful or constructive in the longer run. Trusting audiences, and opening space for them – it's more than one kind of door that needs opening after all. (Brine and Keidan, pp. 28–9)

Of course, not all of Forced Entertainment's work displays such complete confidence in audiences. The virulent attack upon voyeurism in *Showtime* indicates that the company is deeply concerned with the ethical questions raised by watching spectacles of suffering. But Etchells's emphasis upon trusting audiences is a refreshing departure from the expressions of aggression and anger outlined above. This, hopefully, is indicative of a new direction in performance practice.

What's more, there are signs that programmers and marketing departments may be beginning to trust their audiences in a new way. The desire to engage with audiences and their responses has resulted in the emergence of a new category of work in the United Kingdom in recent years, as venues have begun to host 'scratch nights', where unfinished work is presented and artists have an opportunity to gather feedback from audiences. Some venues are going to extraordinary lengths to develop meaningful relationships with their audiences. For example, the organisers of the Birmingham performing arts festival Fierce! not only have an 'Ambassadors group' of audience members who are formally consulted each year about the festival's programme content, publicity, and marketing but took their engagement with the audience a step further in 2008 when they invited audience members to vote for their favourite show, announcing on their website that they were giving 'you, the audience, the power to program your own festival!' (www.myfiercefestival.co.uk; accessed 31 March 2008).

So there is evidence that audiences are beginning to be trusted by practitioners and by industry. But it seems that theatre scholars have yet to develop this trust. In fact, we have yet to step up to the challenge of addressing the question of what we really know about what theatre does for those who witness, watch, or participate. Before we can do so, we need to challenge the mythologies and disperse some of the mystification which surround responses to theatrical performance. Here, I am certainly in agreement with Rancière, who argues in 'The Emancipated Spectator' that accepting the limitations of representation might be a more useful approach:

> Breaking away from the phantasms of the Word made flesh and the spectator turned active, knowing that words are only words and spectacles only spectacles, may help us better understand how words, stories, and performances can help us change something in the world we live in. (p. 280)

As Rancière indicates, repudiating myths of magical or malevolent transformation does not necessarily involve rejecting the idea that the performing arts have agency. Instead, this leave-taking may mean that we get a firmer grasp of the form and function of the interventions they are able to make. Greater engagement with actual audiences would certainly help theatre scholars understand how and why audience members do not experience the manipulation central to hugely popular theatre events such as the *Blue Man Group* as 'torture' – *pace* Lyn Gardner – but as pleasurable, or 'amazing, funny, different … hilarious … very clever', as theatre-goers on the Ciao product review website put it (http://travel.ciao.co.uk/Blue_Man_Group_New_London_Theatre__6546231; accessed 27 December 2008). Ignoring responses like these means that we are failing to take them seriously.

Performance practice also offers those currently charged with delivering the numerous governmental initiatives designed to widen participation in the arts, education, the social services and local government a vivid and valuable illustration of the problems and potentials of audience (or 'ordinary' people's) participation. On the one hand, theatre sometimes shows us that much of what passes for participation is nothing of the sort. Performances which ostensibly invite the audience to make a creative contribution, only to offer them the choice of option A or option B – or the chance to give responses which are clearly scripted by social and cultural convention – are as disappointing and mendacious, in their own way, as political consultation exercises which merely provide an illusion of public dialogue while serving to legitimate decisions taken by the authorities. On the other hand, there are signs that theatre can provide meaningful forms of audience participation and engagement. Realising these, however, involves learning to trust audiences and offering them real choices; giving them a sense of ownership, or the opportunity to make a meaningful contribution to the work's development. It requires careful planning, long-term commitment, great sensitivity, and an acceptance that genuine participation has risks as well as potential rewards. Theatre practitioners need to acknowledge that participation can be profoundly disturbing; that it may involve making ourselves vulnerable as we open ourselves to unexpected experiences and outcomes. They surely also need to give participants the space to reflect upon the limitations of creative or political agency. These are principles which politicians and policy-makers who want to harness the power of participation and the will of 'ordinary' people would also do well to bear in mind.

further reading

The writings of theatre and performance practitioners determined to change the relationship between theatre and audience are the most stimulating place to begin reading in this area. The central role of the audience in early twentieth-century theatrical experimentation is well reflected in the manifestos and essays of Artaud, Marinetti, and Brecht, collected respectively in *The Theatre and Its Double* (1981), *Let's Murder the Moonshine* (1991), and *Brecht on Theatre* (2001). Grotowski's *Towards a Poor Theatre* (1991) and Barker's *Arguments for a Theatre* (1998) are testimony to the ongoing interest in active audiences among theatre-makers, and McGrath's *A Good Night Out* (1981) and Boal's *Theatre of the Oppressed* (1979) are excellent examples of approaches to the audience which explicitly address the connections between experiences of community and theatre. For a snapshot of the British theatre industry's current preoccupation with audience development, see Brine and Keidan's *Programme Notes* (2007).

Bennett's *Theatre Audiences* (1990, revised 1997) remains an extremely useful starting-point within a more academic approach, not least because the book is a central reference point for others working in the field. The section on 'Spectators and Audiences' in Balme's *The Cambridge Introduction to Theatre Studies* (2008) provides an effective, up-to-date summary of trends in audience research. All of Kershaw's publications, which range from rigorous analysis of the commodification of the theatrical experience during the 1980s and 1990s to evocative accounts of radical performance, are highly recommended. Blackadder's *Performing Opposition* (2003) is a detailed and insightful historical account of theatre riots and protests across Europe between 1890 and 1930. Knowles's *Reading the Material Theatre* (2004) delivers a convincing demonstration of the contingencies of reception. *The Senses in Performance* (edited by Banes and Lepecki, 2006) analyses a wide range of performances which have sought to engage audiences through touch, taste, smell, sight, and sound.

Auslander's *Performance: Critical Concepts in Literary and Cultural Studies* (2003) contains essays by Blau, De Marinis, Rayner, and Ubersfeld which provide excellent— though sometimes challenging – examples of the application of literary, psychological, and philosophical theories.

In addition, Carlson's *Theories of the Theatre* (revised 1993) provides an insightful and detailed description of a range of theoretical approaches to the study of theatre audiences. For those interested in gauging the extraordinary range of methodologies in theatre studies, Phelan's poetic 'On Seeing the Invisible' (2004) and Davis and Emeljanow's *Reflecting the Audience* (2001), which marshals an impressive array of facts and figures, are good representatives of opposite ends of the spectrum. Readers who are interested in following up Bennett's suggestions for sources of quantitative data may look to the reports provided by the Society of London Theatres, the Broadway League, and the Wallace Foundation on their websites. At the time of writing, these are www.solt.co.uk, www.broadwayleague.com, and www.wallacefoundation.org.

The study of audiences in other disciplines can also be illuminating. Theatre is notable by its absence from *The Audience Studies Reader* (2003), edited by Brookner and Jermyn, but this collection provides a valuable summary of historical and contemporary approaches to audience in cultural studies. Aaron's *Spectatorship* (2007) provides an up-to-date, accessible introduction to some of the issues raised by film theory. *Participation* (2006), a collection of essays from a visual arts perspective edited by Bishop, contains a thought-provoking introduction as well as Eco's 'The Poetics of the Open Work' and Kaprow's 'Notes on the Elimination of the Audience'. All three essays engage valuably with the question of how we respond to art and performance.

Aaron, Michele. *Spectatorship: The Power of Looking On*. London: Wallflower, 2007.

Abercrombie, Nicholas, and Brian Longhurst. *Audiences: A Sociological Theory of Performance and Imagination*. London: Sage, 1998.

Adams, Matt, Steve Benford, and Gabriella Giannachi. 'Pervasive Presence: Blast Theory's Day of the Figurines.' *Contemporary Theatre Review* 18.2 (2008): 219–35.

Adorno, Theodor, and Max Horkheimer. *Dialectic of Enlightenment*. London: Allen Lane, 1973.

Alasuutari, Pertti, ed. *Rethinking the Media Audience*. London: Sage, 1999.

Artaud, Antonin. *The Theatre and Its Double*. Trans. Victor Corti. London: John Calder, 1981.

Auslander, Philip, ed. *Performance: Critical Concepts in Literary and Cultural Studies*. London: Routledge, 2003.

Balme, Christopher B. *The Cambridge Introduction to Theatre Studies*. Cambridge: Cambridge UP, 2008.

Banes, Sally, and André Lepecki, eds. *The Senses in Performance*. London: Routledge, 2006.

Barish, Jonas. *The Antitheatrical Prejudice*. Berkeley and London: U of California P, 1981.

Barker, Howard. *Arguments for a Theatre*. 3rd ed. Manchester: Manchester UP, 1998.

Barker, Martin. 'Reviews.' *Participations* 1.2 (2004). 20 September 2005 <http://www.participations.org/volume%201/issue%202/1_02_ blackadder-kattwinkel_review.htm>.

Barthes, Roland. *Image–Music–Text*. Trans. Stephen Heath. London: Fontana, 1977.

Beckerman, Bernard. *The Dynamics of Drama: Theory and Method of Analysis*. New York: Alfred A. Knopf, 1970.

Bennett, Susan. *Theatre Audiences: A Theory of Production and Reception*. Rev. ed. London: Routledge, 1997.

Bennett, Susan. 'Theatre Audiences, Redux.' *Theatre Survey* 47.2 (2006): 225–30.

Berkoff, Steven. *Free Association: An Autobiography*. London: Faber & Faber, 1997.

Bishop, Claire. 'Antagonism and Relational Aesthetics.' *October* 110 (2004): 51–79.

Bishop, Claire, ed. *Participation*. London: Whitechapel; Cambridge, MA: MIT Press, 2006.

Blackadder, Neil. *Performing Opposition: Modern Theater and the Scandalized Audience*. Westport, CT: Praeger, 2003.

Blau, Herbert. *The Audience*. Baltimore, MD: Johns Hopkins UP, 1990.

Boal, Augusto. *Theatre of the Oppressed*. London: Pluto, 1979.

Bourriaud, Nicolas. *Relational Aesthetics*. Trans. Simon Pleasance and Fronza Woods. Dijon, France: Les Presses du Reél, 2002.

Brecht, Bertolt. *Brecht on Theatre*. Ed. and trans. John Willett. 2nd ed. London: Methuen, 2001.

Brine, Daniel, and Lois Keidan, eds. *Programme Notes: Case Studies for Locating Experimental Theatre*. London: Live Art Development Agency, 2007.

Brook, Peter. *The Empty Space*. 1968. London: Penguin, 1990.

Brookner, Will, and Deborah Jermyn, eds. *The Audience Studies Reader*. London: Routledge, 2003.

Carlson, Marvin. 'Theatre Audiences and the Reading of Performance.' *Interpreting the Theatrical Past*. Eds. Thomas Postlewait and Bruce McConachie. Iowa City: U of Iowa P, 1989. 82–98.

Carlson, Marvin. *Theories of the Theatre*. Rev. ed. Ithaca, NY: Cornell UP, 1993.

Davis, Jim, and Victor Emeljanow. *Reflecting the Audience: London Theatregoing, 1840–1880*. Hatfield, UK: U of Hertfordshire P, 2001.

Davis, Tracy C., and Bruce McConachie. Introduction. *Theatre Survey* 39.2 (1998): 1–5.

De Marinis, Marco. 'Dramaturgy of the Spectator.' *TDR* 31.2 (1987): 100–14.

Diamond, Elin. 'The Violence of "We": Politicizing Identification.' 1991. *Critical Theory and Performance*. Eds. Janelle Reinelt and Joseph R. Roach. Rev. ed. Ann Arbor: U of Michigan P, 2007. 403–12.

Eco, Umberto. *The Role of the Reader: Explorations in the Semiotics of Texts*. Bloomington: Indiana UP, 1979.

Etchells, Tim. *Certain Fragments: Contemporary Performance and Forced Entertainment*. London: Routledge, 1999.

Fish, Stanley. *Is There a Text in This Class?* Cambridge, MA: Harvard UP, 1980.

FitzPatrick Dean, Joan. *Riot and Great Anger: Stage Censorship in Twentieth-Century Ireland.* Madison: U of Wisconsin P, 2004.

Frank, Thomas, and Mark Waugh, eds. *We Love You: On Audiences.* Frankfurt: Revolver Blanco, 2005.

Goldberg, RoseLee. 'Here and Now.' *The Artist's Body.* Ed. Tracey Warr. London: Phaidon, 2000. 246.

Grotowski, Jerzy. *Towards a Poor Theatre.* 1968. London: Methuen, 1991.

Handke, Peter. *Offending the Audience.* 1966. Plays: 1. London: Methuen, 1997.

Heddon, Deirdre, and Jane Milling. *Devising Performance: A Critical History.* Basingstoke, UK: Palgrave Macmillan, 2006.

Iser, Wolfgang. *The Act of Reading: A Theory of Aesthetic Response.* Baltimore, MD, and London: Johns Hopkins UP, 1978.

Jackson, Anthony. *Theatre, Education and the Making of Meanings.* Manchester: Manchester UP, 2007.

James, Henry. *The Tragic Muse.* London: Macmillan, 1890.

Jauss, Hans Robert. *Toward an Aesthetic of Reception.* Trans. Timothy Bahti. Minneapolis: U of Minnesota P, 1982.

Kattwinkel, Susan, ed. *Audience Participation: Essays on Inclusion in Performance.* London: Greenwood, 2003.

Kershaw, Baz. *The Radical in Performance: Between Brecht and Baudrillard.* London: Routledge, 1999.

Kershaw, Baz. 'Oh! For Unruly Audiences! Or, Patterns of Participation in Twentieth-Century Theatre.' *Modern Drama* 42.2 (2001): 133–54.

Klaver, Elizabeth. 'Spectatorial Theory in the Age of Media Culture.' *New Theatre Quarterly* 11.44 (1995): 309–21.

Knowles, Ric. *Reading the Material Theatre.* Cambridge: Cambridge UP, 2004.

Lancaster, Kurt. 'When Spectators Become Performers and Theater Theory: Contemporary Performance-Entertainments Meet the Needs of an "Unsettled" Audience.' *Journal of Popular Culture* 30.4 (1997): 75–88.

Mackintosh, Iain. *Architecture, Actor and Audience.* London: Routledge, 1992.

Marinetti, F. T. 'The Pleasure of Being Booed.' *Let's Murder the Moonshine: Selected Writings. 1911–15.* Ed. R. W. Flint. Trans. R. W. Flint and A. A. Coppotelli. Los Angeles: Sun and Moon, 1991. 122.

McGrath, John. *A Good Night Out: Popular Theatre: Audience, Class and Form.* London: Eyre Methuen, 1981.

Merleau-Ponty, Maurice. *The Phenomenology of Perception.* 1945. 2nd ed. Trans. Colin Smith. London: Routledge, 2002.

Mills, Fiona. 'Seeing Ethnicity: The Impact of Race and Class on the Critical Reception of Miguel Piñero's *Short Eyes*.' *Captive Audience: Prison and Captivity in Contemporary Theater.* Eds. Thomas Fahy and Kimball King. London: Routledge, 2003. 41–66.

Mulvey, Laura. *Visual and Other Pleasures.* London: Macmillan, 1989.

Olsen, Christopher. 'Theatre Audience Surveys: Towards a Semiotic Approach.' *New Theatre Quarterly* 71 (2002): 261–75.

Phelan, Peggy. 'On Seeing the Invisible: Marina Abramović's "The House with the Ocean View".' *Live: Art and Performance.* Ed. Adrian Heathfield. London: Tate Publishing, 2004. 17–27.

Puchner, Martin. *Stage Fright: Modernism, Anti-theatricality, and Drama.* Baltimore, MD, and London: Johns Hopkins UP, 2002.

Rancière, Jacques. 'The Emancipated Spectator.' *Artforum International* 45.7 (2007): 271–80.

Rayner, Alice. 'The Audience: Subjectivity, Community and the Ethics of Listening.' *Journal of Dramatic Theory and Criticism* 7.2 (1993): 3–24.

Reason, Matthew. 'Young Audience and Live Theatre, Part 1: Methods, Participation and Memory in Audience Research.' *Studies in Theatre and Performance* 26.2 (2006): 129–45.

Reason, Matthew. 'Young Audience and Live Theatre, Part 2: Perceptions of Liveness in Performance.' *Studies in Theatre and Performance* 26.3 (2006): 221–41.

Rebellato, Dan. *1956 and All That: The Making of Modern British Drama.* London: Routledge, 1999.

Report from the Joint Select Committee of the House of Lords and the House of Commons on the Stage Plays (Censorship) together with the Proceedings of the Committee, Minutes and Appendices. London: Government Publications, 1909.

Ridout, Nicholas. *Stage Fright, Animals and Other Theatrical Problems.* Cambridge: Cambridge UP, 2006.

Sandford, Mariellen, ed. *Happenings and Other Acts*. London: Routledge, 1995.

Sauter, Willmar. *The Theatrical Event: Dynamics of Performance and Perception*. Iowa City: U of Iowa P, 2000.

Savran, David. *Breaking the Rules: The Wooster Group*. New York: Theatre Communications Group, 1988.

Schechner, Richard. *Environmental Theater*. New York: Hawthorn, 1973.

Shepherd, Simon. *Theatre, Body and Pleasure*. London: Routledge, 2006.

Stanislavski, Constantin. *An Actor Prepares*. Trans. Elizabeth Reynolds Hapgood. London: Methuen, 1988.

Stefanova, Kalina. *Who Keeps the Score on the London Stages?* Amsterdam: Harwood Academic Publishers, 2000.

Tulloch, John. 'Approaching Theatre Audiences: Active School Students and Commoditised High Culture.' *Contemporary Theatre Review* 10 (2000): 85–104.

Tulloch, John. *Shakespeare and Chekhov in Production and Reception: Theatrical Events and Their Audiences*. Iowa City: U of Iowa P, 2005.

Ubersfeld, Anne. *L'École du spectateur: Lire le théâtre 2*. Paris: Éditions Sociales, 1981.

Ubersfeld, Anne. 'The Pleasure of the Spectator.' Trans. Pierre Bouillaguet and Charles Jose. *Modern Drama* 25.1 (1982): 127–39.

Wagner, Anne M. 'Performance, Video, and the Rhetoric of Presence.' *October* 91 (2000): 59–80.

Yeats, W. B. *Explorations*. New York: Macmillan, 1962.

index

Abramović, Marina, 23–4, 62–3
Acconci, Vito, 50
anti-theatrical prejudice, 38–42, 72
applause, 19–21
Artaud, Antonin, 17, 27, 77
audience:
    active engagement of, 3, 25, 27,
        46–9, 55–76
    antagonism towards, 2, 4, 9, 46,
        49–52
    community within, 6–9
    definitions of, 2–3, 5
    energy among, 7, 10–11
    frustration with, 2, 47–9, 54–5
    individual members of, 5–6,
        9–10
    methodological analysis of, 19,
        22–3, 25, 28–31, 37
    participation in performance,
        55–76
    passivity of, 16–17, 27, 51–3
    production of, 31–2

    suspicion of, 4, 8, 9, 15, 37–45
    trusting of, 72–4, 76

Barker, Howard, 52–4, 77
Bennett, Susan, 3, 12–13, 15, 25,
    28–30, 78–9
Blackadder, Neil, 26–7, 46, 78
Blast Theory, 67–72
Blue Man Group, 64–5, 70, 75
Boal, Augusto, 56, 58–9, 77
Bourriaud, Nicolas, 59–61
Brecht, Bertolt, 17, 26, 46–9, 77

cultural studies, 27–8, 79

Etchells, Tim, 1–2, 6–8, 52,
    72–3

Gardner, Lyn, 57–8, 65, 75
Grotowski, Jerzy, 1, 67, 77

Handke, Peter, 1, 2, 51–2

Jarry, Alfred, 26, 46

Kershaw, Baz, 19–21, 25,
    63–4, 78

Living Theatre, the, 51, 63–4

marketing, 29–32, 73–4
Mulvey, Laura, 13–14

performative writing, 23–5
Phelan, Peggy, 23–5, 62–3, 79
Piñero, Miguel, 9
Pinter, Harold, 13
Punchdrunk, 65–6

Rancière, Jacques, 15–17, 74–5
reader response theory, 11–13, 15
Relational Art, *see* Nicolas
    Bourriaud
responses:
   affective, 22–5, 53
   interpretive, 6, 12–13, 17–18, 53

physiological, 10, 18–20, 23–5,
    27, 53
reviewing, 4, 8–9, 33–6
riots, 25–7, 78

Shunt, 66
spectator, *see* audience
spectatorship, theories of, 13–14,
    15–17, 29, 56, 64,
    74, 79
stage fright, 43–4
Stein, Gertrude, 45

technology, developments in, 14,
    19, 69–70
television studies, 11, 14, 28–9
Theatre in Education, 56, 61

voyeurism, 2, 13–14, 52, 73

Wooster Group, the, 17–18

Yeats, W. B., 44

Theatre& small books on theatre & everything else

NEW FOR 2010...

978-0-230-57548-6

978-0-230-21871-0

978-0-230-57462-5

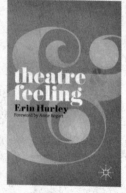

978-0-230-21846-8

978-0-230-22064-!

'Palgrave Macmillan's excellent new outward-looking, eclectic *Theatre*& series. These short books, written by leading theatre academics, do much to reintroduce some of the brightest names in theatre academia to the general reader.' - Guardian Theatre blog

theatre& small books on theatre & everything else

PUBLISHED IN 2009...

theatre & the city
Harvie
978-0-230-20522-2

theatre & politics
Joe Kelleher
978-0-230-20523-9

theatre & human rights
Paul Rae
978-0-230-20524-6

theatre & the body
Colette Conroy
978-0-230-20543-7

'Short, sharp shots' for theatre students and enthusiasts
Presenting the best writing from A-list scholars
Vibrant and inspiring

theatre & audience
Freshwater
978-0-230-21028-8

theatre & globalization
Dan Rebellato
978-0-230-21830-7

theatre & ethics
Nicholas Ridout
978-0-230-21027-1

theatre & education
Helen Nicholson
978-0-230-21857-4

Place your order online at www.palgrave.com